A JOURNALIST LOOKS AT
THE PARABLES

ANGELO MONTONATI

A JOURNALIST
LOOKS AT
THE PARABLES

 St Paul Publications

Original title: *L'Anticamera del Regno*
Copyright © 1990 Edizioni Paoline, s.r.l., Cinisello Balsamo, Italy

Translated by Deborah Misuri Charkham

Cover design by Diane Edward

St Paul Publications
Middlegreen, Slough SL3 6BT, United Kingdom

English translation © St Paul Publications UK 1991

ISBN 085439 385 4

Printed by The Guernsey Press Co. Ltd, Guernsey, C.I.

St Paul Publications is an activity of the priests and brothers of the Society of St Paul who proclaim the Gospel through the media of social communication

Contents

Foreword 7

Introduction 11

The Word of God 17
  The sower

The enemy 26
  The good seed and the weeds

The day of reckoning 34
  The parable of the talents

God's love and justice 43
  The labourers in the vineyard

The First World, the Third World
and God 51
  The rich man and the poor man

You never had it so good 59
  The rich fool

Christian attitude to money 64
  The shrewd manager

Celebrating death 71
  The bridesmaids

An invitation from God   78
     The wedding banquet

Love betrayed   86
     The tenants of the vineyard

God's patience   94
     The unforgiving slave

God never says no   102
     The parable on prayer

True confession   107
     The Pharisee and the tax collector

Appearances are deceptive   114
     The two sons

Ninety-nine against one   119
     The lost sheep

The logic of love   126
     The prodigal son

Who is my neighbour?   135
     The good Samaritan

Foreword

Of the 17 parables interpreted here by Angelo Montonati, the one I have always found most difficult is the parable of the talents. Matthew's report that more will be given to those who have, and that those who have nothing will lose even that which they have, has always struck me as outrageously unjust. I have heard these quotes taken out of context and used in support of some of the worst materialist excesses we have witnessed during the last decade.

This author examines this and the other parables in the proper context, that of the loving and forgiving nature of Jesus Christ. 'It is a mistake to bury ourselves in laziness', he says. How easy it is to be satisfied with little, to put off until tomorrow what we can do today. Procrastination is just a multi-syllabic definition of sloth. As a journalist who loves the thrill of writing for a daily paper, I need often to examine my motives, and question myself as to whether I am putting my own talents to their best use.

The word comes from the Greek *parabolé*, a comparison or placing beside, but parables are more than allegories or moral tales. I find they have a disconcerting habit of burying themselves deep in my memory and popping up didactically at inconvenient moments, such as when I see the tenth homeless youngster begging for money on the London underground on a single journey passing through King's Cross, or when the tax inspector insists I owe him £1,000 more than I think I do.

In the New Testament we read that the secret of the Kingdom of God is given to the disciples, but to the outsider everything is in parables. A parable can be interpreted by all but only fully understood by an elite, in Christ's case his disciples, chosen partly because they had the ears to hear. The outsider must look and yet not see, listen and listen and still not understand. If the outsider understood, he would turn to God and repent, and God would forgive him (Mark 4:10-12). As I struggle to comprehend this enigmatic riddle, I conclude that suffering must come before understanding, and the worst solution would be not to try.

Christ's parables are the most famous, but there are others in the Old Testament which deserve a mention. One of my favourites, because it is one of the most chilling, concerns David and his wife Bathsheba, formerly the wife of his officer Uriah the Hittite. As related in 2 Samuel 11-12, David fell in love with Bathsheba after he witnessed her taking a bath, and sent Uriah into the front line of battle where he was killed. So God sent the prophet Nathan to David, and Nathan told the king a parable of a rich and a poor man in the same town.

The rich had many cattle and the poor had one lamb, who was like a daughter to him. When a visitor arrived at the rich man's home, he killed the lamb to feed him. David, outraged, at first threatens to kill the rich man then recognises himself in the tale and repents. Montonati in this book writes of the extraordinary continuation of language from the time of Christ to the present day as exemplified in the parables. How much more extraordinary is it then that parables can speak to us even from the time of David, 1000 years before.

In giving us these simple stories, rich in meaning, Christ gave our priests a device that can be heard being deployed from pulpits across England to this day. Philosophers and writers enriched by the parable include Kierkegaard, Kafka and Camus. Yet the distressing fact to be accepted is that parables like that of Lazarus, the starving, infested beggar denied even the leftovers from the rich man's table but carried off by angels to be with Abraham, have been with us for nearly 2000 years, and there are beggars still on the streets of London.

Christ's parables are fictitious but true to life. They embody ideas and, though spoken nearly 2000 years ago, apply with equal force to our secular, modern life. They are at once revelatory and mysterious. They illustrate, as vividly as the Sermon on the Mount, that the rule of God applies on earth as in heaven. Properly studied, they grant enticing insight to how we can proceed to find heaven on earth. They show this heaven is not

9

where we might be tempted to think it is: in riches, power and physical gratification; but in communion and identification with outcasts and sinners, tax collectors and the poor, as witnessed by Christ himself.

RUTH GLEDHILL
Religious Affairs Correspondent,
The Times

Introduction

I have written not as an interpreter of the Scriptures, but as a journalist of today. So even though these lines have been revised by an expert to avoid any heresy or nonsense, the reader will find that they contain a personal approach and interpretation which should be taken at face value: spontaneous input aimed at stimulating some thought about faith.

The parables of Jesus – to be regarded as his own words and memorised by the apostles – are the most extraordinary example of the continuation of language that I know. They are also a fine lesson for the journalist. The "carpenter's son", as they called him in Nazareth, wanted to be understood by everyone. This behaviour is the exact opposite of that of many famous people today, who address themselves to an aware audience of intellectuals, and mainly for their own benefit.

Whenever Jesus opened his mouth, his words made straight for the minds and hearts of the people, from the most humble to the learned Pharisee. This explains the success of his preaching. The thronging crowd forced him to jump on a boat in the lake and push himself a few metres off shore so that he was able to continue. And his words were so fascinating that the crowd even forgot to eat. One day Jesus had to feed thousands of people by miraculously multiplying some loaves of bread and a few fish which a prudent boy had brought from home.

The parables gave me the cue to discuss some very current issues. They are made-to-measure stories for life and the history of our times. They arouse not just our intelligence but also, and above all, our willingness. Because God's word must flourish within us and persuade us to change something in our lives. This I hope will happen in myself as well as in my readers.

Most of the parables – from a certain viewpoint, all of them – are based on the kingdom of heaven. Jesus creates flashes of light and glimmers of happiness, but he always makes sure we understand that nothing is given to us for free. From time to time, he himself sets the standards of behaviour and conditions of merit; and he proposes how we should avail ourselves of help when difficulties and enemies block our path. The anxiously waiting Father (presented perhaps as a king, a master or a wealthy man) emerges from this countless number of proposals as a severe figure but, aching with love for humanity, he is ready to rejoice every time a son rejects sin, repents and returns to him. Here we notice the twofold aspect of the Gospel parables: the eschatological (the kingdom as the final goal of our existence); and the historical (all the incidents occurring during the course of this life of ours, the anteroom of the kingdom).

Jesus touches on all the various aspects of his peoples' daily life in order to make us understand our final destiny. He makes reference to farmers, shepherds, housewives, merchants and fishermen. He is most concerned that the message gets through to everyone in a comprehensible way, giving priority to the "small" the poor, the illiterate and the humble who are the prime candidates for the kingdom. There is plenty for everyone.

"You, farmer, do you know what the kingdom resembles? A grain of mustard, the smallest of seeds which, once grown, becomes so big that the birds seek shelter among its branches." What a fine message of hope! We are reminded of the missionaries who spread the faith in the very places where it seemingly could not be welcome, but where God's grace makes it grow in countless hearts. One person sows, another reaps.

"To you, housewife, I say that the kingdom is like the yeast a woman adds to three measures of flour to make it rise." Once again this hidden faith, the minority (three to one the parable says), is capable of making the world's dough "rise". The Gospel may appear to be alien, falling on deaf ears, but our society is still full of the goodness of this yeast. During the first stormy student demonstrations of 1968, the Vice Chancellor of an Italian university said: "Don't be afraid, the world is full of saints!"

"You, aimless vagrant, do you know what the kingdom resembles? Treasure buried in a field. A man finds it by accident and sells everything he possesses and buys that field. His days of searching are over." Leave everything behind – the kingdom is worth it.

"You, merchant, listen to me: the kingdom is like a man looking for precious pearls who, having found an extremely valuable one, sells everything he has and buys it." As if to say that the best business deal you can make in life is to make sure you have God's friendship. This alone – like that sole pearl – is worth more than anything else.

To the fishermen he says: "The kingdom of heaven is like a net cast into the sea to catch all sorts of fish. When it is full, the fishermen haul it ashore. Then they sit down to sort the fish, putting the good ones in the baskets and throwing away the bad ones. So it will be at the end of the world: the angels will come and separate the evil from the good and throw them into the burning furnace, where there will be weeping and gnashing of teeth."

Everyone figures in the parables as we shall see: kings, servants, masters, honest and dishonest managers, judges, porters, children at play, widows, nubile girls, thieves, plunderers, tax collectors, priests, debtors and creditors, bricklayers, tailors and wine merchants, fathers, good and bad sons. The entire world.

We journalists also get a mention. This discovery is made on the assumption that we are allowed to be included with the scribes (in truth, not very well-liked by Jesus). In fact when the spinning myriad of images of the kingdom ceases, the Teacher appears to offer us an invitation: "Every scribe, with knowledge of the kingdom of heaven, is like a man of property who finds both new and ancient things among his riches."

He compares us to men of property. Well... are we or are we not the "fourth estate"? And the "riches" are made up of words – quite a precious commodity. I have thought long and hard about this phrase and the possible content of the riches. The new things are the news which professional duty obliges us to report, but in conjunction with the ancient things, the unchangeable and constantly valid principles and values. Both transient and eternal truth. Perhaps Jesus wanted to tell me this: firstly, collect background information about faith, then talk about it using "new words" but never betraying the Word, the Truth. This is what I have tried to do in these pages.

The
word of God

Jesus began to teach beside the sea. Such a very large crowd gathered around him that he got into a boat on the sea and sat there, while the whole crowd was beside the sea on the land. He began to teach them many things in parables, and in his teaching he said to them: "Listen! A sower went out to sow. And as he sowed, some seed fell on the path, and the birds came and ate it up. Other seed fell on rocky ground, where it did not have much soil, and it sprang up quickly, since it had no depth of soil. And when the sun rose, it was scorched; and since it had no root, it withered away. Other seed fell among thorns, and the thorns grew up and choked it, and it yielded no grain. Other seed fell into good soil and brought forth grain, growing up and increasing and yielding thirty and sixty and a hundredfold." And he said, "Let anyone with ears to hear listen!"

When he was alone, those who were around him along with the twelve asked him about the parables. And he said to them, "To you has been given the secret of the kingdom of God, but for those outside, everything comes in parables; in order that

> 'they may indeed look, but not
>   perceive,
> and may indeed listen, but not
>   understand;
> so that they may not turn again and be
>   forgiven.'"

And he said to them, "Do you not understand this parable? Then how will you understand all the parables? The sower sows the word. These are the ones on the path where the word is sown: when they hear, Satan immediately comes and takes away the word that is sown in them. And these are the ones sown on rocky ground: when they hear the word, they immediately receive it with joy. But they have no root, and endure only for a while; then, when trouble or persecution arises on account of the word, immediately they fall away. And others are those sown among the thorns: these are the ones who hear the word, but the cares of the world, and the lure of wealth, and the desire for other things come in and choke the word, and it yields nothing. And these are the ones sown on the good soil:

they hear the word and accept it and bear fruit, thirty and sixty and a hundredfold."

(Mark 4:1-20)

When Jesus spoke he attracted a crowd because the language he used was not the complicated and often incomprehensible language of intellectuals. It was more the language of a poet or narrator or, if you like, of a journalist. Like a true teacher, he always made himself understood by everyone and the crowds never tired of listening to him.

Mark the evangelist introduces his account of the parable of the sower with the visual detail: "Once again he began to teach on the seashore. The crowd gathered around him was so enormous that he had to go aboard a boat where he sat, afloat on the water, while the crowd remained on land along the shore." A fantastic image: a beach on Lake Tiberias (which the Gospel calls a "sea" as the amphitheatre, and a boat as the stage for Jesus.

This is perhaps the "key" parable for under-standing Jesus and his strategy towards people. I really like this idea. I also like it because it speaks of the word, the message: it is the mass media parable. And its importance is so great that, having been related in the Gospel, there has to be a detailed explanation – a sign that it is the starting point for understanding the rest.

A farmer goes out to sow his seeds. We picture him straight away. He is a "law unto himself", a real character. He scatters the seeds in all directions, very wastefully for a farmer. By doing this, some of the seed ends up on the road and the birds waste no time in pecking it up. Some of it falls among the stones and is unable to put down solid roots, so the shoots are soon dried up by the sun. Other seeds wind up in among the thorn-bushes which strangle the ears of corn as soon as they grow. Finally, those seeds which happen to fall on fertile, well-prepared soil flourish in abundance and multiply thirty, sixty or a hundred times over.

This means that the sowing season comes to all of us and is, therefore, a meeting with God's truth because – as Jesus himself explains – this farmer is the heavenly Father and the seed is his word. He spreads it everywhere without exception. He does not discriminate. We, on the other hand, are free to choose between being a road, stones, thorn-bushes or fertile soil. It depends on our reaction.

These words are not just limited to Christians. In one way or another all people receive good seed, the hidden God who speaks to the conscience. If we study the various religions in the world, we come across many admirable examples of honesty, faith and love in humankind. So many flashes of truth! Just as an example, think of Mahatma Gandhi, the apostle of non-violence. Just think of the deep sense of the sacred that pervades many people whom we consider to be primitive but whose cultures maintain precious values which the "advanced", colonising West has in fact lost!

It's true to say that God's voice rings out more

loudly, clearly and frequently, on every street corner, for us Christians. Even though we live in a secular community, we cannot avoid now and then running into seed-messages wanting to sprout in our consciences. We therefore have a greater responsibility and fewer excuses.

But we are often not even aware of God's great gift to us. We remain indifferent and distracted by the thousands of other messages bombarding us. We are like the road: everything passes over us. Can a seed sprout in asphalt? Obviously not.

Sometimes we find ourselves actually refusing: the ability to reject our Creator, disobey him and resist his love is the great mystery of human freedom. I know people who close the door (politely, of course, but they still close it) on a priest who has come to bless their house. They are "not interested". God is for the underdeveloped. He is alien and makes no sense to this type of person. This seed is eaten up by the birds which, in Jesus' explanation, symbolise Satan who "comes and takes it all away". We are reminded of the policies of certain countries where atheism is law, aimed at making the mind and heart insensitive and impervious to God's message. Apparently they are succeeding (or are they?). This is also the case where parents do not wish their children to receive religious education, and ask for them to be excused from Scripture lessons at school.

Or else, we behave like the stones: at first we joyfully welcome the word. But it is a passing enthusiasm, a habit. We don't allow it to take root inside us. We are fickle. One or two trials and tribulations are all that are needed to knock us down and make us forget everything. Then, more likely than not, we probably get angry with the Lord for putting us to the test.

Many people can tell the same story: they start out well with baptism, religious knowledge, first communion and confirmation, perhaps even a monastic or convent school education. But, once they become adults, the very moment they should be honouring their faithful duties, religion for them becomes something only fitting for children. They lack the courage to openly admit that they go to Mass on Sundays (if indeed they still go). Or else they look for reasoned arguments like: "I communicate with God in my own way... what need is there for priests?" The Church – although unequalled when it comes to the experiences of life – is not considered to be up to it.

An obvious inferiority complex replaces the facts and figures of religion. The dominant culture conditions them; more notice is taken of the words of lay "ascetics" whose popularity rating is always higher than the Pope's. Here is an excellent example: in 1968 when Paul VI published the encyclical *Humanae Vitae*, many people (and not only among "the laity") accused it of being culturally behind the times. These days we realise that this document was extremely prophetic. The Pope had sensed the ever diminishing importance of human life in our society. In fact, crime, drugs, terrorism, abortion, contraception, homosexuality, euthanasia are unfortunately becoming ever increasing realities in the news and in the custom of our times (some of these are even presented as "victories for civilisation").

That's the way it is. By behaving like stones, we end up by living a Godless existence. Or perhaps we do have the odd bit of nostalgia for "when I was a child and served as an altar-boy..."

Sometimes our inner feelings are those of fertile soil, but not as well-tended as it might be. The seed of the holy word cohabits with the weeds, the fruits of bad seed. In this way thorns can suffocate the ears of corn and prevent them from flourishing. The weeds are the counter-messages with which the consumer society continually fills our eyes and ears – messages travelling in the opposite direction from that of the Gospel. Jesus says: "Blessed are the poor." Mass media advertising replies: "Blessed are the rich, the beautiful, the successful with loads of money." Jesus says: "Blessed are those who weep." Have we gone crazy? Blessed are those who enjoy themselves, even at someone else's expense... All we need do is read the newspapers to realise which people most readers consider to be important: millionaire football players and film and TV actors. Even if they lead dissolute lives, all is forgiven and their vices almost become virtues...

In his explanation, Jesus says that the thorn-bushes are the "world's worries, the illusion of wealth and all other desires". There is emphasis on the word "illusion" when referring to wealth, a recurring theme in many parables.

And finally there is the fertile soil: that part of humanity which opens itself with sincere commitment to the word of God and puts it into practice. Here, Jesus creates some categories based on yield: thirty, sixty and one hundred per cent, depending on our willingness. The saints are those who yield one hundred per cent. Their response to the Lord is immediate and total, to the point of sacrificing life itself. Some respond violently. Think of the countless conversions that have enriched the history of the Church. They do a thorough cleansing job on their souls, ploughing deeply to eradicate every weed. Like Zacchaeus, Paul of Tarsus (St Paul), Augustine of Hippo, Francis of Assisi, Ignatius of Loyola,... A long list, continuously enriched by new names.

For others, the love of God is spontaneous. Its intensity is great enough to make them renounce everything for his sake. Catherine of Siena, Teresa of Avila, Thérèse of Lisieux,... All these examples show the results which an unconditional "yes" to the Lord can produce.

As I said before, this is also the parable of mass media and journalists. Journalists are the professionals when it comes to words (either written or spoken). They contribute to the spreading of messages, good or bad. Our responsibility is as rewarding as it is grave. We can instil hope and love in people just as we can nudge them towards distress and hatred. However, you readers also have a responsibility, because of the choice of newspapers and the selection of television channels. We need to know how to make an intelligent and courageous choice. There's no lack of good press, and these days the sower uses this above all to scatter his good seed. To ignore this (as some Christians do, out of fear of what other people might say) means that we are allowing the thorn-bushes of the parable to grow inside us. Choosing and supporting it is the first step towards showing that we take God seriously. It is a guarantee that the good soil of our soul will be fertilised, and the reaper will be rewarded with an excellent harvest.

The enemy

PARABLE OF THE GOOD SEED AND THE WEEDS

Jesus put before them another parable: "The kingdom of heaven may be compared to someone who sowed good seed in his field; but while everybody was asleep an enemy came and sowed weeds among the wheat, and then went away. So when the plants came up and bore grain, then the weeds appeared as well. And the slaves of the householder came and said to him, 'Master, did you not sow good seed in your field? Where, then, did these weeds come from?' He answered, 'An enemy has done this.' The slaves said to him, 'Then do you want us to go and gather them?' But he replied, 'No; for in gathering the weeds you would uproot the wheat along with them. Let both of them grow together until the harvest; and at harvest time I will tell the reapers, collect the weeds first and bind them in bundles to be burned, but gather the wheat into my barn.'"

Then he left the crowds and went into the house. And his disciples approached him, saying, "Explain to us the parable of the weeds of the field." He answered, "The one who sows the good seed is the Son of Man; the field is the world, and the good seed are the children of the kingdom; the weeds are the children of the evil one, and the enemy who sowed them is the devil; harvest is the end of the age, and the reapers are angels. Just as the weeds are collected and burned up with fire, so will it be at the end of the age. The Son of Man will send his angels, and they will collect out of his kingdom all causes of sin and all evil-doers, and they will throw them into the furnace of fire, where there will be weeping and gnashing of teeth. Then the righteous will shine like the sun in the kingdom of their Father. Let anyone with ears listen!"

(Matthew 13:24-30;36-43)

We already know that the sower is generous and patient with his field (the human race). But – and this is the interesting part of this parable – he is not the only one to sow seeds. He has an enemy who, by concentrating his attention on the fertile soil where God's word can yield a hundredfold, is not so much disputing the ownership of this property but the use that is made of it. There is

27

something else, of equal importance: he is not interested in those who are indifferent or wishy-washy about matters of faith. They may not know it, but they are already his.

Those who do interest him are the people who are sincerely trying to put the teachings of the Gospel into practice. It is no accident that the saints are often the devil's prime targets for assault and battery. A whole wealth of literature on this subject has drawn the attention of scholars. This is the dark side of mystical experience.

So, what does the enemy do? At night, when everyone is asleep, he goes out to sow weeds in the same place where good grain has been sown. To illustrate evil, Jesus purposely chose the sprouting of these bogus ears of wheat, known also as tares, which proliferate and take vital nourishment from the wheat.

This Gospel story is lacking in any graphic details. It sticks to the bare essentials, almost as if leaving entirely up to us the job of working out each step of the enemy's furtive trespassing into the field that does not belong to him. In journalistic language, the heart of the matter can be found with the five words, 'who, where, when, how and why' – the basic ingredients for any news story.

So, "who"? This is the first question. We have already said it: the character mentioned now and then in church, the devil, the ultimate rebel, the anti-Christ, he who weaves the plot of evil in the world by exploiting humankind's weakness.

Some of you may laugh and say that it's the same old witch hunt, a thing of the Middle Ages.

These days we prefer to ridicule the idea of the devil. We even say that a harmless and kind-hearted person is "a good devil..."

And yet, during his public audience in November 1972, Paul VI, a great and complex pope who was more alert than most to the doubts of modern humankind, had already come out with this extremely clear phrase: "Evil is not just an insufficiency, but a living being who is spiritual, corrupted and a corrupter. A terrible reality. Mysterious and fearful. Anyone who refuses to recognise his existence steps outside the framework of biblical and ecclesiastical teaching. Some make him out to be a separate issue which does not, like all other creatures, originate from God. Some explain him as a pseudo reality, a conceptual and imaginary personification of the unknown causes of our afflictions." And again on 13 August 1986, John Paul II returned to this discussion: "Prince of this world, Beelzebub, Belial, Foul Spirit, Tempter, Evil One and, lastly, anti-Christ. He is compared to a lion, a dragon and a snake. The Scriptures tell us so."

However, the existence of demons is a maxim of Christian faith. Of course, we are not talking of the devils depicted in Mediaeval or even modern paintings up to the time of the Second Vatican Council, but of spiritual entities which influence people's spirit and will, leading them into error and pushing them towards evil. We all experience this daily. Even Jesus was tempted by the devil when he went into the wilderness to pray. Ignoring this important episode would be the same as quoting the Gospel only when it's convenient.

It goes without saying that doctrine concerning the devil automatically draws from that on angels: the Church would never suggest our daily recital of that beautiful prayer, the *Angelus,* if these spirits placed next to us by divine goodness to counterbalance devilish influences were imaginary characters. Unfortunately, we often find people confusing Bible stories with the likes of *Snow White and the Seven Dwarfs*, forgetting that, at least once a year in the parish (usually when celebrating the Easter Vigily liturgy, confirmation or first communion), the baptismal promises are renewed. "Do you reject Satan and all his works and empty promises?" And we reply: "I do". It's true that the secular press laughs at this, but this is also part of the plan: in fact, the devil's cleverest trap is to convince people that he does not exist. However, current affairs confirm just the opposite. Let's flick through the newspapers: the unmentionable offences, mounting crime, the dominance of a corrupt society contrary to fundamental human and Christian values are all realities that mask a very able "government". The apostle John was driven to say, "the whole world is subjected to the power of the Evil One", confirming the presence of Satan throughout human history.

Now we know "where" the devil works. Let's try to see "how" and "when". Jesus said: "At night, while we are all asleep..." Evil is never done in broad daylight. It needs the complicity of darkness, like deception – at which the devil is the true master. When we throw up our hands in

30

horror over certain events in our society we never think that these could also be the consequences of our "sleep". If, for example, the press, radio and television or theatre in general are continuing to inject poison into peoples' consciences, it is also due to the laziness of those who should be fighting against it. "The children of darkness are cleverer than the children of light" is the explanation offered by Jesus himself.

Finally we come to the "why". And this is the crux of the matter. God allows the good and the bad to co-exist on an equal footing, but doesn't it sometimes seem that the bad have the upper hand? When a good person dies, you often hear: "Couldn't the Lord have taken a delinquent in his place?" This very complaint was made to the heavens by poor Job, a just man at the nadir of his misfortune. And yet the message in this parable is very clear: there is room for everyone in this world, the good and the bad. It is not our place to discriminate. In fact, the Christian should love everyone equally and, if he is to show some preference, it should be towards his enemy.

As always, divine logic is the opposite from ours. The Creator respects individual freedom pushed to the point of rebellion (and the devil is nothing other than a rebel spirit). He is patient with the wicked and permits them to work day by day by the side of the just. This is difficult for us to understand. If we look at life-styles in certain countries of the world, where small, wealthy, forceful minorities prosper by exploiting millions of poor people and crushing their most fundamental rights, we are tempted to resort to immediate radical solutions.

The same temptation was felt by the sower's servants who, were amazed by what had happened. "How can it be," they asked him, "that there are tares among the wheat? Did you not scatter good seed?" A naive attempt to blame God for what had happened. Then they said: "Do you want us to pull up the weeds?" The answer: "No, because while pulling up the weeds you might also uproot the wheat."

This is a definite "no" to any sort of indiscriminate violence that always creates innocent victims and which, in the long run, never pays. Gandhi had understood. We can also verify this by following world political events. It is always the poor who suffer from the ravages of the most bloody wars. Tyrants and their accomplices always have an escape route and a Swiss bank account. We could easily name some in Africa, Asia and Latin America as well as Europe.

However, God's patience does have its limit. Sooner or later the scene will change. We are assured of this by the Lord of our history. "Let them grow together until harvest time", said the sower. In other words, the day of reckoning, a subject so often referred to by Jesus in his sermons. It is all written in the Book of Life, nothing is lost and the Lord's accounts always balance.

The Teacher goes into detail when describing the end of the world and the day of judgement. "The Son of Man will send his angels who will gather up all the sins and evil-doers from his kingdom and throw them into the burning furnace where there will be much crying and gnashing of teeth. Then the just will shine like the sun in their Father's kingdom. Listen, then, if you have ears to hear with!" The last phrase is an energetic reminder of our mentality today: so reluctant to listen to talk of judgement, heaven and hell... No man is so deaf as he who does not want to hear. And yet, reality is that which the Gospel describes. Evil-doers will be sent to their just destination, and the "enemy" will be vanquished forever.

Meanwhile we, here on earth, are a mixture of wheat and tares. Let us take note and be aware of that which awaits us. The true lesson learned from this parable is "responsibility". We live in a world that has lost its sense of sin and personal responsibility. It seems that there is collective blame for all evil. This will result in collective absolution without distinction: the murderer with the gentleman, the guilty with the innocent. And, above all, it will result in the confusion of truth with error, with not seeing even though we have eyes and not hearing even though we have ears. Exactly as Jesus said – quoting Isaiah – just before he told the parable of the tares: "You will hear, but you will not understand; you will look, but you will not see. Because the hearts of this people have hardened..."

The day
of reckoning

"A man, going on a journey, summoned his
slaves and entrusted his property to them; to
one he gave five talents, to another two, to
another one, to each according to his ability.
Then he went away. The one who had received
the five talents went off at once and traded
with them, and made five more talents. In the
same way, the one who had the two talents
made two more talents. But the one who had
received the one talent went off and dug a
hole in the ground and hid his master's money.

After a long time the master of those slaves
came and settled accounts with them. Then
the one *who* had received the five talents came
forward, bringing five more talents, saying,
'Master, you handed over to me five talents;
see, I have made five more talents.' His master said to him, 'Well done, good and trustworthy slave; you have been trustworthy in a
few things, I will put you in charge of many

34

things; enter into the joy of your master.' And the one with the two talents also came forward, saying, 'Master, you handed over to me two talents; see, I have made two more talents.' His master said to him, 'Well done, good and trustworthy slave; you have been trustworthy in a few things, I will put you in charge of many things; enter into the joy of your master.' Then the one who had received the one talent also came forward, saying, 'Master, I knew that you were a harsh man, reaping where you did not sow, and gathering where you did not scatter seed; so I was afraid, and I went and hid your talent in the ground. Here you have what is yours.' But his master replied, 'You wicked and lazy slave! You knew, did you, that I reap where I did not sow, and gather where I did not scatter? Then you ought to have invested my money with the bankers, and on my return I would have received what was my own with interest. So take the talent from him, and give it to the one with the ten talents.

For to all those who have, more will be given, and they will have an abundance; but from those who have nothing, even what they have will be taken away. As for this worthless slave, throw him into the outer darkness, where there will be weeping and gnashing of teeth."

(Matthew 25:14-30)

As they were listening to this, he went on to tell a parable, because he was near Jerusalem, and because they supposed that the kingdom of God was to appear immediately. So he said, "A nobleman went to a distant country to get royal power for himself and then return. He summoned ten of his slaves, and gave them ten pounds, and said to them, 'Do business with these until I come back.' But the citizens of his country hated him and sent a delegation after him, saying, 'We do not want this man to rule over us.' When he returned, having received royal power, he ordered these slaves, to whom he had given the money, to be summoned so that he might find out what they had gained by trading. The first came forward and said, 'Lord, your pound has made ten more pounds.' He said to him, 'Well done, good slave! Because you have been trustworthy in a very small thing, take charge of ten cities.' Then the second came, saying, 'Lord, your pound has made five pounds.' He said to him, 'And you rule over five cities.' Then the other came, saying, 'Lord, here is your pound. I wrapped it up in a piece of cloth, for I was afraid of you, because you are a harsh man; you take what you did not deposit, and reap what you did not sow.' He said to him, 'I will judge you by your own words, you wicked salve! You knew, did you, that I was a harsh man, taking what I did not deposit and reaping what I did not sow? Why then did you not put my money into the bank? Then when I returned, I could have collected it with interest.' He said to the bystanders, 'Take the pound from him and give it to the one who has ten pounds.' (And they said to him, 'Lord, he has ten pounds!') 'I tell you, to all those who have, more will be given; but from those who have nothing, even what they have will be taken away. But as for these enemies of mine who did not want me to be king over them – bring them here and slaughter them in my presence.'"

Luke 19:11-27

This parable seems to sing the praises of the businessman. It talks of investments, capital and interest rates. However, the "deal" in question has nothing to do with the business world; it is about our life or, to be more exact, the use we should make of it.

So, we have an employer who, before leaving on a long trip, asks three of his employees to report to him and gives them a sum of money to invest. To one he gives five talents; to another two, and one talent to the third. To make it easier for us, just imagine that one talent equals about five thousand pounds. To each of them according to his ability. This means that we are all born with equal rights as people, but we are different in other respects. For this reason, we can't expect everyone to produce at the same rate. It is a principle of social justice: those with more must give more, and only on this condition is there a right to earn proportionally more. Countries where there is real socialism are aware of this. These countries thought that they could form a perfect society of "equals" by levelling the salaries out without taking individual productivity into account. The results were disastrous. In practice there were those who became "more equal" than others, leading to the advent of the meritocracy.

The argument is perhaps clearer in Luke's story which runs parallel to this parable (Luke 19:11-27). Here, the employer is nothing less than a prince and he has ten employees. However, they all receive an identical sum of money. The first earns ten times the sum and, as a reward, is nominated governor of ten cities; the second gains five times as much and becomes governor of five cities; the third, however, is punished for having kept his money hidden in a handkerchief.

But let's get back to our story. The first employee gets to work straight away and invests the money in a deal that doubles his capital. He is obviously more on the ball than the others which is probably why the employer gives him the biggest slice to look after – twenty-five thousand pounds.

But the second employee doesn't waste any time either, and his ten thousand become twenty. The third, on the other hand, is more laid back. "The boss," he thinks, "is going to be away for quite a while, so what's the hurry?" So, having dug a hole in a secret corner of his garden, he buries the money.

Matthew does not go into detail, but we have no difficulty today in imagining how the good-for-nothing spends his day: he sleeps late, stays up until all hours with his friends in the bar and enjoys life. He is probably a spoilt brat, with no financial worries and comes from one of those families who don't bother to teach their children to take responsibility for their future or to prepare them for earning their own living. After all, the future is very secure. Even his job (no doubt given to him by friends in high places) does not occupy much of his time. In current terms, absenteeism is probably a policy he adopts.

But the moment of truth comes to us all.

"After a long time," the evangelist says, "the employer returns home and begins to go over the accounts with his employees." Clearly, the employer's trip is in fact our voyage, our very existence from the moment we reach the age of reason and can make our own responsible choices.

The meeting is short. The first employee arrives: "You gave me twenty-five thousand pounds, and I have doubled it. The second says: "Your ten thousand pounds have become twenty." "Good", says the employer, visibly pleased, "you have been faithful with small matters, I will give you something more important. Come and share your lord's joy!"

He changes his tune with the third employee. We can sense that there has always been bad blood between the two of them. "I knew", the good-for-nothing says arrogantly, trying to justify himself, "that you are a hard man, who reaps where he has not sown, and harvests where he has not tilled. I was afraid and so I buried your money to hide it. Here, I am returning it to you."

The employer is furious when he hears these excuses which, among other things, show a total lack of imagination. Anyone else would at least have thought of putting the money in the bank, and the employer reprimands him: "You evil, good-for-nothing servant! So you think I reap where I do not sow and harvest where I do not till. In that case, you should have put my money in the bank so that when I returned I could have collected the interest as well as the money!"

There is a dramatic conclusion, an unusually harsh sentence. "Go," says the employer, "and give the talent to the person who has ten of them. Because, as the proverb says, he who has much will receive even more and will be in abundance. He who has little will lose that small amount which he has. Throw out this useless servant, out into the darkness. There he will weep desperately!"

It may seem surprising that the best employee also receives the money given to his unfortunate colleague. But this is not a normal contract of employment. And the opposing party is the Employer with a capital "E" who, when we are about to embark upon the great adventure of our life, entrusts us with talents which – we must never forget – are his property. Our job is to make them grow. This is something intimately connected with ourselves, almost a secret genetic code, the embryo of a project which we must develop to its fullest. A certain personality, a varying degree of intelligence, an iron constitution or delicate health, a family, material wealth: this is our bag and baggage when we come into the world, and it is unevenly distributed (the "ability" of which the Gospel speaks). Some are at a disadvantage when compared to others, but that does not matter. The important thing is to make the most of what has been given to us.

These days, the "me" and "mine" culture leads us to believe that we can do as we please with our own lives and that of others: our bodies, time, the environment, the earth's natural resources. But everything is on loan. It makes no sense, therefore, to congratulate ourselves on being as handsome as Alain Delon or as great a footballer as Maradona. And despairing because we're not is equally useless. We must accept ourselves for what we are, and make the most of it. It is a mistake to "bury ourselves" in laziness. The disaster for many of today's people is their preference for a drug-induced "trip" rather than daily commitment. They are either despairing or condemned to despair.

Investing the talents means living our life day after day, starting from the smallest things. The "good and trustworthy" servants mentioned in the Gospel did not do anything special. What their employer appreciated about them was their faithfulness "in small matters".

The employer is very exacting. At times he

could well give the impression that he reaps where he doesn't sow, to use the good-for-nothing's words. But perhaps we are the ones who don't know how to look within ourselves and discover God's plan. We prefer to envy others (the grass is always greener on the other side!). Life today has its problems. We are not permitted to live on a private income. This is not one of those TV quiz shows where we can choose whether to take the prize-money or gamble it further in the hope of doubling the amount. Here, the person who takes the money is condemned.

It is perhaps no accident that the Gospel speaks of doubling. It means that God goes halves with us. He is the first to put down his half; we have to put down ours. "Heaven helps those who help themselves" is another popular proverb.

Lastly, a coincidence: the parable ends with the dramatic scene of the Day of Judgement, the final day of reckoning when the Son of Man who, seated on his throne, separates the just from the wicked. We therefore know what to do in order to deserve these words which the King will address to the just: "Come, you who have been blessed by my Father. Enter the kingdom that has been prepared for you since the time of the creation of the world."

God's
love and justice

PARABLE OF THE LABOURERS IN THE VINEYARD

"The kingdom of heaven is like a landowner who went out early in the morning to hire labourers for his vineyard. After agreeing with the labourers for the usual daily wage, he sent them into his vineyard. When he went out about nine o'clock, he saw others standing idle in the marketplace; and he said to them, 'You also go into the vineyard, and I will pay you whatever is right.' So they went.

When he went out again about noon and about three o'clock, he did the same. And about five o'clock he went out and found others standing around; and he said to them, 'Why are you standing here idle all day?' They said to him, 'Because no one has hired us.' He said to them, 'You also go into the vineyard.' When evening came, the owner of the vineyard said to his manager, 'Call the labourers and give them their pay, beginning with the last and then going to the first.' When

43

those hired about five o'clock came, each of them received the usual daily wage.

Now when the first came, they thought they would receive more; but each of them also received the usual daily wage. And when they received it, they grumbled against the landowner, saying, 'Those last worked only one hour, and you have made them equal to us who have borne the burden of the day and the scorching heat.' But he replied to one of them, 'Friend, I am doing you no wrong; did you not agree with me for the usual daily wage? Take what belongs to you and go; I choose to give to this last the same as I give to you. Am I not allowed to do what I choose with what belongs to me? Or are you envious because I am generous? So the last will be first, and the first will be last.'"

(Matthew 20:1-16)

This parable talks about trade union members (the labourer, the unemployed, the person on the dole) in Jesus' time. However, this boss' attitude towards his workers would certainly not please today's employers. Here, in fact, it seems that levelling of wages, sweet idleness, arrogant ruling classes, unrewarded professionalism and productivity are considered worthy of praise. The usual Gospel paradox – in accordance with Jesus' logic which is completely the opposite of ours.

And yet, true trade unionists could end up by appreciating this logic, when considered in relation to the kingdom, the life to come, rather than a normal contract of employment (for reasons to be explained later).

So, we have a wealthy landowner who has a big vineyard. Presumably it is spring pruning time, or even harvest time. In any case, he needs hands. When morning breaks, the boss leaves home to recruit some day-labourers. The scene is reminiscent of depressed areas in some countries today: the unemployed gather in the central square, waiting for the "foreman" to arrive and sign on the strongest. Matthew specifies that it is dawn and there are already people waiting. The boss agrees the wages. They accept and go to the vineyard.

Evidently, however, there are not enough of them so, at nine o'clock, the man goes back to the square to get more help together; then again at midday and at three o'clock and five o'clock in the afternoon which is almost knocking-off time. And yet he still finds willing hands even at that hour. The pay, however, is a bit vague: "I will give you whatever is right" says this odd person who seems to favour the lazy ones who were the last to go to the square. However, he asks an important question to the five o'clock group: "Why have you been idly hanging around here all day?" Their answer: "Because no-one took us on for the day." Try to question any passer-by about the poor and starving in the Third World. You may well be told that many of these people find themselves in this state because they don't want to work. Unfortunately, this saying about "Southerners" or the Third World is still heard today in some areas of advanced European countries. No one stops to think that this obvious psychological weakness when faced with effort often conceals a centuries-old heritage caused by insufficient nourishment, lack of hygiene, no knowledge of their rights, exploitation by the powerful and so on. A Brazilian, Indian or African labourer definitely cannot withstand the same duress as a multivaccinated, well nourished, politically protected European trade union member who works five or, at most, six days a week and enjoys a restful annual holiday.

Underneath the apparent laziness there lies the disarming reply to the boss in the parable: "No one took us on." Modern society is cruelly selective: in the name of productivity and profit, priority must be given to the youngest, healthiest and strongest. If he is male, all the better, because the female with her monthly cycle or, worse, pregnancy, takes more sick leave and costs the company more.

All the drama of unemployment therefore surfaces in that reply. Those who haven't experienced it cannot possibly understand. Put yourself in the shoes of a jobless parent with children to look after; or of a handicapped person, someone who is blind, often obliged to live off charity. There has often been no other choice than "idly hanging around". Sometimes this is a prelude to the only avenue left open – making the most of any opportunity – and then crime can be just around the corner.

However, let's get on with Matthew's story. At sunset, the owner of the vineyard tells his foreman to pay the workers. "But," he adds to everyone's surprise, "start with those who began at five o'clock."

The situation immediately becomes difficult. The blood pressure rises when they see that priority is given to the late-comers. "How can it be?" some of them say. "They have only worked for an hour and you have treated them the same as us when we have worked all day long in the heat." In itself, there's not a flaw in this argument.

The boss hears this and calls one of the protesters (a union leader?). "Friend (this is what he calls him, so his language is not that of the class struggle), I am not doing you wrong. Did we not agree on the usual daily pay? Take your money and go. And if I choose to give the last to arrive the same as I have given you, can I not do as I wish with what is mine? Or are you jealous because I am good?" He finished with a statement which, for the listeners gathered around Jesus (above all the ever-present Pharisees), had the same effect as a punch in the stomach: "In this way the last will be first, and the first last."

If we read between the lines, the plot thickens a bit. First and foremost, we once more see the emergence of the absolute freedom with which God, more than ever Lord, can act. That which seems unjust to us simply means that he saves us not because of our merits but because of his good-

47

ness and grace. A grace conceivable only as a gift, not as the result of a contract. In this way, his kingdom is open to the world at large, even outside the circle of "the righteous" if this is the correct term for the good. It is open to the hardened sinners who, called at the last moment, perhaps even on their death-beds, welcome the invitation and repent.

The meeting with the vineyard owner could happen at any time (the theme is repeated from a different angle in other parables). God goes out to look for people at any time and in any place. For example, Saul of Tarsus, the future St Paul, did not receive his invitation in the town square among the waiting unemployed (in his own way he was "employed" in fighting against Jesus). It was received with violence after he had been thrown from the saddle by blinding light. In the case of the good thief, on the other hand, one of the "late-comers", a glance and an appeal to Jesus on the cross was all that was needed to extract the reassuring promise: "Today you will be with me in paradise." How true it is that every human story is a mystery in itself.

The first labourers to be taken on, however, were not complaining about the pay, but about the different treatment given to the others. It is here that God's logic becomes clear: all people are equal when it comes to rights. The differences are levelled out. Luckily, there is no class structure nor any "connections" of any kind in his kingdom. If any classification does exist – and the Gospel is clear on this! – it is the opposite of anything down here, in the disconcerting grading of "beatitudes".

The behaviour of the discontented labourers contains one of the greatest of our vices: envy. They are disappointed because the others have been favoured. It never crosses their minds that the boss' decision, justice apart (or with different parameters from ours), is an expression of generosity. In that moment, justice is formulated on the basis of personal opinion and nothing else.

We come across it every day: we find it difficult to congratulate a colleague who has been promoted to a higher grade, getting ahead of us. A worrying question bores its way into our minds: "Why him and not me? Who knows what tricks he's used to get ahead..." Envy is the very tendency not to accept ourselves for what we are, not to accept what life has to offer, for better or worse. In other words, the grass is always greener on the other side.

The Gospel doesn't mention any comments made by the five o'clock labourers, who must have been pleasantly surprised by their pay. They were most probably very grateful for the favour. Not necessarily, however. Gratitude is not a very common virtue. Nevertheless, we have to think about it.

The moral of our story is that the owner of the vineyard asks us to work for him. Having been baptised, there's no doubt that the vast majority of us belong to the first shift (the dawn workers) and, therefore, to the discontented group who put forward their claims. We need to look on the positive side of this situation which, contrary to appearances, is where its merits lie. The parable aside, from the moment we come into the world we have the extraordinary gift of grace. The problem is how to keep this gift, make it flourish and honour our calling. Then, if others join in along the way, there can only be greater joy. The more workers there are in the vineyard, the better. Gratitude, therefore, is a must. Every day we should thank God for having created us and made us Christians.

Then, joy. To be the first to be called by the Father means that he loved us first. We should think seriously about the great fortune of our baptism, with which the owner of the vineyard has grafted us into the family of those called to eternal happiness; to an infinitely greater "pay" than the wages agreed for our day's labour on earth.

The First World,
the Third World, and God

PARABLE OF THE RICH MAN AND THE POOR MAN

"There was a rich man who was dressed in purple and fine linen and who feasted sumptuously every day. And at his gate lay a poor man named Lazarus, covered with sores, who longed to satisfy his hunger with what fell from the rich man's table; even the dogs would come and lick his sores.

The poor man died and was carried away by the angels to be with Abraham.

The rich man also died and was buried.

In Hades, where he was being tormented, he looked up and saw Abraham far away with Lazarus by his side. He called out, 'Father Abraham, have mercy on me, and send Lazarus to dip the tip of his finger in water and cool my tongue; for I am in agony in these flames.'

But Abraham said, 'Child, remember that during your lifetime you received your good things, and Lazarus in like manner evil things; but now he is comforted here, and you are in agony. Besides all this, between you and us a great chasm has been fixed, so that those who might want to pass from here to you cannot do so, and no one can cross from there to us.'

He said, 'Then father, I beg you to send him to my father's house – for I have five brothers – that he may warn them, so that they will not also come into this place of torment.' Abraham replied, 'They have Moses and the prophets; they should listen to them.' He said, 'No, father Abraham; but if someone goes to them from the dead, they will repent.' He said to him, 'If they do not listen to Moses and the prophets, neither will they be convinced even if someone rises from the dead.'"

(Luke 16:19-31)

This is a surprising *identikit* of modern consumer society. There are three protagonists: the rich man, the poor man and God.

The rich man is sketchily but succinctly described: "he dressed in purple and fine linen" (the most valuable fabric of the day). He was one of those people who renew their wardrobe every season and only wear designer clothes. A successful person, the classic, up-to-the minute socialite.

"He feasted sumptuously every day." We have now identified a person who is used to caviar, champagne and top restaurants. A first emphasis must be placed on the words "every day". They have a purpose (there are no superfluous words in the Gospel). We are, unfortunately, made well aware of the fact that many people on our planet are dying of hunger: millions of them every day. There are children who don't reach the age of five because of lack of food. Newspapers and television show us the faces of poverty in Third World countries. And yet we still don't fully comprehend that we, in the well-to-do industrial North, are the rich gluttons. With our calorie intake, we are over-fed. Our rich meals often lead us to suffer from liver and heart trouble and we need to resort to diets to regain our figures. We have even made an art and a science out of eating. We call it "gastronomy".

Then there is the poor man. The Gospel gives him a name, Lazarus (contrary to custom in today's society, where only the illustrious surnames are mentioned, the rich man is anonymous). He is a ragged beggar, seated near the palace door in the hope that someone will bring him a few leftovers.

Lazarus is the image of that Third World we mentioned earlier. His body is covered with sores. Malnutrition, dirt, the lack of a home or any comforts explain his condition. Today, Lazarus lives in the "townships" and hovels on the outskirts of great cities. He sleeps on park benches or makeshift cardboard beds in railway stations. As he has no-one to care for him, when he dies his body is taken to the anatomy department of medical schools to be dissected by students.

Lazarus waits for someone to take him something, but no one thinks about it and the left-overs are thrown in the rubbish bin to be devoured by stray cats and dogs. Perhaps a kind-hearted "charwoman" could have sneaked something out to him (there is always a sense of solidarity among the poor), but the Gospel doesn't mention it. It does, however, say that "even the dogs licked his sores". Jesus could not have given greater praise to "man's best friend". In this particular case, the dogs had a greater sense of humanity than many a rich human intellect.

So Lazarus has nothing. Even though his only desire is to relieve his hunger with left-over scraps from the rich man's table. He had no revolutionary intentions of upsetting the *status quo*. He was content just to survive. But the rich man's heart is hard. Poverty is offensive to the "well-off". "What does this old tramp want?" might have been his irritated comment.

A thought: "left-overs" are exactly what the current so-called "international economic structure" gives to the poor. And if they complain, they are beaten. Some statistics: 1,700 million people in the world do not reach the age of 60; 1,500 million receive no medical attention; 1,000 million live in abject poverty; 2,000 million have no drinking water; 800 million work like animals and earn less than £100 a year.

These figures were provided by FAO, a United

Nations organisation dealing with food and agriculture. Missionaries can confirm the statistics. They live with them. An example: in Brazil, there are 10 million unemployed, 11 million underemployed, 35 million illiterates, 25 million abandoned minors, 86 million hungry. And all because of unfair distribution of wealth, not only in Brazil but in many countries on earth.

The poor man died and was carried by the angels to be with Abraham. A splendid image to be fully enjoyed by those with the gift of faith. Proof of there being a sense to innocent suffering, and that no tear is ever shed in vain.

"Then the rich man also died." Death has no use for money and is afraid of no-one. "And he was buried", the Gospel adds. The poor man has no grave, but the rich man does and we can even imagine his tombstone bearing the words "noble heart", "kind soul", "a model father" over which his relatives cry inconsolably.

The Gospel does not explain why the glutton goes to hell. It is obviously automatically taken for granted. We are reminded of Jesus' curses: "Cursed are the rich, for they have already had their comfort; cursed are the sated, for they shall suffer hunger..." There's more to come later.

The anonymous man is still certain of being in time for last-minute repentance. He calls out: "Father Abraham, have pity on me and send Lazarus to dip the tip of his finger in water to wet my tongue, because this flame is torturing me." His words contain all the traditional arrogance of those who are used to being served. He expects

Lazarus to bring him some relief. Abraham replies bitterly: "My child (this is what he calls him because, deep down, he feels sorry for the man's unhappy ending), remember that you have received all that is good during your lifetime, while Lazarus has only had the bad. And now he is consoled, while you are in the midst of torment." And he adds: "What is more, there is a great abyss between you and us: those who want to come to us cannot, nor can we come to you." This is the final condemnation. The rich man insists that Lazarus should at least be sent to tell his five brothers. Who knows... perhaps an apparition could convert them. Abraham finds this request superfluous: "They have Moses and the prophets. They should listen to them." But the wretched man knows all too well about people like himself. He knows that they couldn't care a whisker about the prophets and the law. It's the same story even today.

We have had saints in the past, and we still have them today: Mother Teresa of Calcutta, Bishop Helder Camara, the American Dorothy Day, Archbishop Desmond Tutu, the missionaries fighting for human rights, the freedom fighters (the real ones, not the caricatures). They all raise their voices in defence of those who have no voice. However, very little notice is ever taken. The West insists on squandering billions on arms; we are forced to consume more and more under the banner of a mistaken "quality of life", forgetting that not very far away there are people dying of hunger.

"If they do not listen to Moses and the prophets," Abraham concludes, "they would not be persuaded even if someone was raised from the dead."

The dialogue ends at this point. What follows belongs to God's infinite mercy. Quite frankly, I find it hard to think about the eternal unhappiness of hell, and to admit that the abyss of evil – the product of weak and imperfect creatures – can force the abyss of divine love – the absolutely perfect maker – to lock the sinner out forever. But without doubt, divine judgement has a different logic from ours.

Nevertheless, the dramatic story of Lazarus still reflects the history of humanity. If we listen to Christ, an incredible wealth of treasure is open to us. In fact, in another Gospel passage, we read that whoever gives food and clothing to the poor is, in reality, giving to Jesus himself. Lazarus and those like him become Christ's sacrament, no more and no less than the bread of Holy Communion. Turning a blind eye and pretending not to see when the hungry ask for help is like turning away from him. In other words, a sacrilege.

So where does all this lead? If we take Jesus' words seriously (and his questions are never loaded), our daily way of life must change and the banner we fly will be far more sober. This means we must learn to give up many superfluous things in our lives (that have only become necessities because of constant hammering by advertising, from which we don't know how to escape). We must learn to share and be prepared to help those who are in need. Because the real sin (and the main lesson learned from this beautiful parable) is not being rich, but keeping the wealth all to oneself.

There is a more down-to-earth topic (already touched upon but discussed more fully later) which Jesus develops in the parable of the rich fool in order to prick the conscience by reminding people of their mortality. Fortunately, death does not make allowances for wealth and cannot be avoided with a "pay off".

You never
had it so good

Someone in the crowd said to Jesus, "Teacher, tell my brother to divide the family inheritance with me." But he said to him, "Friend, who set me to be a judge or arbitrator over you?" And he said to them, "Take care! Be on your guard against all kinds of greed; for one's life does not consist in the abundance of possessions."

Then he told them a parable: "The land of a rich man produced abundantly. And he thought to himself, 'What should I do, for I have no place to store my crops?'

Then he said, 'I will do this: I will pull down my barns and build larger ones, and there I will store all my grain and my goods. And I will say to my soul, 'Soul, you have ample goods laid up for many years; relax, eat, drink, be merry.'

But God said to him, 'You fool! This very night your life is being demanded of you. And

59

the things you have prepared, whose will they be?' So it is with those who store up treasures for themselves but are not rich toward God."

(Luke 12:13-21)

Greed and great wealth are often synonymous. We sometimes read newspaper reports about seemingly poor people who leave – perhaps hidden under a mattress – tens or even hundreds of thousands of pounds, the unused fruits of a life of hardship. Or else there are those who think they'll go on forever and never tire of accumulating material possessions, only to pass away without ever enjoying them. We all know that death can be just around the corner: a property tycoon crashes his private jet just as his company is about to reach its greatest moment of economic expansion; a royal pretender to the throne is decapitated by a steel cable while trying out his new skis; a multimillionaire takes too many sleeping pills and never wakes up. Our life hangs by a thread.

Jesus speaks of a miser rolling in money who, after an exceptionally good year, has harvested so much grain that he doesn't know where to put it. His silos cannot contain the quantity, but it never enters his head that the surplus could feed many needy people. He is so gripped by the obsession of "having" that plans for more storage space are his only concern. He is a Scrooge, accumulating his wealth with a view to the definitive "blow out". "Oh soul," he says to himself as he gazes at his cash registers, "you have great reserves of goods, enough for many years; rest, eat, drink and enjoy yourself."

Advertising bombards us with these same messages every day in the papers, on television and on billboards. It focuses on success, measured in accordance with the bank balance, with how much one "has". Our Scrooge's words contain the beliefs of a consumer mentality: the soul (whom he addresses) is only happy when totally absorbed in the thought of money, eating, drinking and enjoying. A common belief. Taking it easy, designer clothes, expensive cars and a menu based on caviar, lobster and champagne is our recipe for happiness these days.

Above all, however, our protagonist is totally unrealistic (it is no accident that Jesus calls him a "fool"). He really believes that he is free to plan his own future. He doesn't think that the Father of time is someone else, whose existence is more forgotten than unrecognised because of today's indifference and materialism.

In fact, with a *coup de théâtre* ripping through the story and turning it into a tragedy, Jesus calls upon God's intervention just at the moment when the miser has set out his plan. The monologue becomes a dialogue with a mysterious interlocutor who passes judgement: "Fool! This very night your life will be taken; then who will get all these things you have kept for yourself?" The curtain now falls and Jesus goes straight to the moral:

61

"This is how it is with those who pile up riches for themselves but are not rich in God's sight."

Further on we find a very important, more detailed and reasoned examination of the "life style" proposed by Jesus to those who want to follow. Firstly there is unlimited opportunity for faith in the very Providence which plans our future: "Do not be worried about the food you need to stay alive, or about the clothes you need for your body," Jesus tells us, "life is much more important than food, and the body much more important than clothes." In other words, eat to live and not vice versa.

After all, God feeds the birds even though they neither sow nor reap, and makes the lilies of the field more elegant than Solomon in all his regal finery. He thinks of us and knows that we have to eat and drink, but he wants us to put his kingdom first (that is to say, he wants us to look on high). The rest will be provided.

This brings us to the final speech, making total sense of the two parables about wealth: "Sell your belongings and give your money to the poor. Provide for yourselves purses that don't wear out, and save your riches in heaven where they will never decrease, for no thief can get to them, no moth can destroy them. For your heart will always be where your riches are."

It's a matter of choosing the right riches. Francis of Assisi taught us an exemplary lesson about this when he made his radical choice in favour of poverty. Many others like him have chosen to receive only the basic necessities from Providence.

A lesson in true democracy is also taught to us by Jesus' followers, those who choose a life of poverty in religious orders and institutes where strict rules bind them, among other things, to a vow of poverty. Regardless of whether they come from a poor background or families laying claim to millions, members of religious orders renounce all personal possessions. The community – often sustained by the generosity of outsiders as well as its members' work – takes care of their necessities, contained within obviously strict limits. Property is not owned but given in use, never as personal possessions and only for the duration of a particular assignment or service.

An attentive and unprejudiced visit to a religious community, be it male or female, could be of great help in understanding many things. Instead of the free market, where profits and personal or national self-fulfilment are the only governing laws, some insight could be gained into how the world could be if economics obeyed the laws of solidarity and Christian love. These are the only laws capable of preventing the anger of the poor from becoming yet another of history's bloody vendettas.

Christian attitude
to money

PARABLE OF THE SHREWD MANAGER

Then Jesus said to the disciples, "There was a rich man who had a manager, and charges were brought to him that this man was squandering his property. So he summoned him and said to him, 'What is this that I hear about you? Give me an accounting of your management, because you cannot be my manager any longer.'

Then the manager said to himself, 'What will I do, now that my master is taking the position away from me? I am not strong enough to dig, and I am ashamed to beg. I have decided what to do so that, when I am dismissed as manager, people may welcome me into their homes.'

So, summoning his master's debtors one by one, he asked the first, 'How much do you owe my master?' He answered, 'A hundred jugs of olive oil.' He said to him, 'Take your bill, sit down quickly, and make it fifty.' Then

64

he asked another, 'And how much do you owe?' He replied, 'A hundred containers of wheat.' He said to him, 'Take your bill and make it eighty.'

And his master commended the dishonest manager because he had acted shrewdly; for the children of this age are more shrewd in dealing with their own generation than are the children of light."

(Luke 16:1-8)

There is a story resembling the many political and legal accounts of our times, where scandalous speculation, private jets, ivory towers, satin bed linen, billion-pound financial crashes are at the forefront of the news. These accounts take up pages and pages of newspaper space, but very rarely do they report any news about the guilty party's sentence. At such dizzy heights, it seems that thieves never work alone. By involving others, they spread the responsibility so thinly that all of them manage to get away with it.

This parable – which shocked the great St Augustine – has a surprise ending: the victim of the robbery shows an incredible sense of fair play when he compliments the thief on his display of shrewdness.

The protagonist of the story is a powerful millionaire who suddenly realises that his accounts are not balancing because his dishonest manager was "wasting his money". By increasing the overheads and other costs, large sums were disappearing.

Having quantified the extent of the "deficit", he summons the man responsible and tells him straight: "Turn in a complete account of your handling of my property, for you cannot be my manager any longer." He is sacked on the spot.

The manager is thrown out and since, in all probability, he will be taken to court, he begins to organise his defence. He is obviously a clever man and not the sort to be easily ruffled. His first consideration is what will happen "after": he is not cut out for farm labour and, after all, working in the fields is far too hard for someone of his standing. He certainly couldn't lower himself to ask others for help. He would be ashamed of having to beg.

Then he has an idea: he will get friendly with his boss' debtors. Perhaps one of them will help him, and welcome him into his home. He calls the first who owes one hundred barrels of oil. The dishonest manager enters fifty into the account ledger and says: "This will take care of it."

The man understands the wink and goes away happily. A second debtor owes a hundred bushels of wheat. This is reduced to eighty and so it goes on with others.

By the time the boss finds out, there is nothing he can do about it. He acknowledges his manager's shrewdness. And Jesus goes on to comment that a lesson can be learned from the people of this world because, in their dealings with each other, "they are much more shrewd than the people who belong to the light."

The story ends here. What follows is open to interpretation, but there is no guarantee that the outcome favoured the dishonest manager who based his plan on the certainty of other people's gratitude. He had vain hopes.

However, our main interest is to analyse some of the rather mysterious words uttered by Jesus immediately afterwards, in praise of honesty and faithfulness, two interlinking virtues: "Make friends through worldly wealth so that when it runs out you will be welcomed in the eternal home."

Point one: worldly wealth means "ill-gotten gains". You can easily make the decision to administer millions without getting your hands dirty. The problem is this: we so easily become attached to money. It can become the most important thing in life. By spending money we live to make money, and we are judged for what we "have" and not for what we "are". This is why newspapers are overflowing with articles about life's "winners" whose victories are measured by the amount of money they have made.

Let's consider those special managerial individuals, the politicians, who are so often criticised for the off-hand way in which they squander (and sometimes appropriate) public money. We need to be faithful with "other people's property", Jesus warns, in order to gain "our own true wealth".

Incidentally, there is one case where politicians

should imitate our manager, even if for a different reason from his. There is a large part of the world – the developing countries, or the "undeveloping" countries as someone called them to give a more realistic view of their poverty-stricken situation – that is deep in debt. These debts are incurred towards the wealthy, industrialised West which often buys up their raw materials at ridiculously low prices, and then sells them manufactured products at prohibitive prices. But if the rich managers sat around a table together with their poor debtors and decided to halve (or even cancel) these debts, then they really would become true friends. Given that the creditors are almost all Christian countries, without doubt this would be an evangelical gesture.

To get back to the parable, the end does not leave believers in any doubt. Point two: worldly wealth is an "alternative" to God. One day Jesus meets a young man from a noble family who asks him what he must do to gain eternal life. "Observe the commandments" is the reply. The young man says: "I have observed them since I was a child." And Jesus replies: "Only one thing is missing. Sell everything you own, distribute it among the poor and you will find treasure in heaven. Then come and follow me". But the young man was "saddened" when he heard these words because he was very rich. Then Jesus added that famous phrase: "How difficult it is for a rich man to enter the kingdom of God! It is easier for a camel to pass through the eye of a needle than for a rich man to enter the kingdom of God."

Lastly, here is a prophecy that still applies to us if we learn to look at things without prejudice: "No one has ever abandoned his home, his wife, his brothers, his parents and his children for the kingdom of God and not received much more on earth, and eternal life forever." As we have said, there is a good reason why Christ's most radical followers are bound by a vow which only permits them to use property but not to own it.

The alternative is stated extremely clearly by Jesus: "No servant can be the slave of two masters: he will hate one and love the other; he will be loyal to one and despise the other. You cannot serve both God and mammon [money]."

Jesus' praise for faithfulness should also be emphasised. He said that those who are faithful in small matters are also faithful when it comes to important matters, and vice versa. Personal honesty begins with everyday trifles: finding a wallet on the road and returning it intact, not skimping on weight when serving a customer, doing your duty in the office even when the boss is away and can't check up on you. This last example can be found in another Gospel parable: "Who therefore is the faithful and prudent manager (the opposite of our earlier example!) whom the master will put in charge of his servants to give each of them, at the established time, their share of food? Blessed is that servant whom the master finds acting in this way when he returns! In truth I say to you, he will be put in charge of all his property. But if that servant were to say to himself: my master is delayed; and he begins to beat the servants and to eat and drink and get drunk, that servant's master will return at a time when he least expects it. He will separate him from the others and he will be put with the unfaithful servants."

With scrupulous faithfulness to her small, everyday duties, St Thérèse of the Child Jesus began her "narrow road" of holiness. In actual fact it is a very crowded motorway along which many, many unacclaimed saints (our parents, the conscientious teacher, the unbiased, scrupulous manager, the punctual and pleasant office-worker, the nurse who puts her heart into helping the sick, etc.) are travelling at high speed towards heaven, perhaps without even knowing it.

Celebrating death

"The kingdom of heaven will be like this. Ten bridesmaids took their lamps and went to meet the bridegroom. Five of them were foolish, and five were wise. When the foolish took their lamps, they took no oil with them; but the wise took flasks of oil with their lamps. As the bridegroom was delayed, all of them became drowsy and slept.

But at midnight there was a shout, 'Look! Here is the bridegroom! Come out to meet him.' Then all those bridesmaids got up and trimmed their lamps. The foolish said to the wise, 'Give us some of your oil, for our lamps are going out.' But the wise replied, 'No! There will not be enough for you and for us; you had better go to the dealers and buy some for yourselves.'

And while they went to buy it, the bridegroom came, and those who were ready went with him into the wedding banquet; and the door was shut. Later the other bridesmaids came also, saying, 'Lord, lord open to us.' But he replied, 'Truly I tell you, I do not know you.' Keep awake therefore, for you know neither the day nor the hour."

(Matthew 25:1-13)

I have always liked Matthew's story – with all its suspense and without the tragic inevitability found elsewhere because it presents death (and this is its theme) as a celebration like "going to meet the bridegroom". This is the true Christian interpretation of the event for those who believe in "life in the world to come".

One immediately imagines how the saints died, with no sadness or despair, but with expressions of joy. In Rome, in the Tor de Specchi monastery a short distance from the Capitol Hill (Campidoglio), where the Oblates of Mary live, a stupendous fresco by Antoniazzo depicts the passing of St Francesca Romana. It shows the woman sitting on a bed, absorbed in prayer, while her soul is being welcomed into the arms of Christ. There is a carpet of flowers between the two images and, on the right, an orchestra of angels play to welcome the newcomer to life in heaven.

And closer to our time there is Dominic Savio, a pupil of Don Bosco's Oratory. He was only fourteen when he passed away with a smile on his lips, exclaiming: "I have never seen anything so beautiful!"

This "mad desire" to meet Christ is a characteristic of the saints. Sickness, suffering, separation from loved ones, even martyrdom; everything else falls into second place. We can therefore understand why, in the language of the heavenly Register Office, the day they die is considered to be the day of their birth into eternal life.

And yet, when we speak of death we evoke one of the greatest "taboos" of modern society where, it is believed, all taboos have been eliminated by science and technological progress. Death is a forbidden word, never to be uttered. If someone does let it slip unintentionally, it then has to be exorcised with the most banal imprecations like "touch wood" and so on. Because death is unquestionably only a misfortune, in fact "the" misfortune par excellence for the modern, materialistic culture and something to be kept at arm's length by turning to superstitions. As if crossing your fingers, or not walking under a ladder, or not letting a black cat cross your path, or not leaving for a trip on Friday the 13th is all that is needed to avert it.

In any event, this idea should be rejected. Visiting a hospital is all that is needed to be convinced that this "fear" has infected just about everyone, with the terrible consequences we all know. No one has the courage to tell the patient the truth about his condition when it reaches its terminal stage. The dying patient is isolated from the rest of the world. People must never find out that it is not always possible to be cured and they might just leave hospital in a horizontal position.

This mentality also pervades the Church. For years now, the catechism lessons seem to have forgotten the eschatological themes, the so-called science of the four last things: death, judgement, heaven and hell. Furthermore, these days we seldom see a priest at the bedside of the sick or accompanying them to the great passing.

Having digressed, let's get back to the parable which is set in the late afternoon. As is still the custom in the villages in the Middle East, once the singing, dancing and games are over, the marriage feast can begin any time after sunset. By torchlight, the bride is led to the bridegroom's house. Later on he is the last to arrive, preceded by a footman, and then the marriage contract is sealed. The women wait for him outside the house. In some villages the procession moves from the bride's house to the groom's just before midnight, after which the celebration begins.

Ten girls wait for the groom. Five of them are considered "wise" and five "foolish". This percentage is rather too optimistic. It's nine o'clock. Nothing's happening. Night has fallen and the crickets are chirping. Jesus leads us to understand that there is no precise time for this type of meeting. For this reason, the five wise girls have brought along some extra oil for their lamps. However the others didn't think of it.

Ten o'clock. Still nothing. Some of the girls fall asleep, tired of waiting. At eleven one of the girls, keeping watch, thinks she sees some lights moving in the distance. "Perhaps it's him. Yes, it is him! Let's get ready." They want to touch up their make-up and make themselves beautiful for the party. "Oh no, our oil has run out," exclaim the five foolish girls. "Give us some of yours, otherwise our lamps will go out!" "Impossible", the others reply. "We'll all end up with no oil. Run and buy some, there's still a shop or two open..."

While they go off, a voice announces the arrival of the procession from a curve in the road: "The groom, the groom!" The doors are opened and the party begins. The five wise girls go inside with the guests. It is midnight. In his story, Jesus chooses this time and, even today, it is used in thrillers to create a sense of mystery and fatality. The darkest hour: as if to remind us that we know nothing at all about death. However, there is the safety of the house where everything is lit up and buzzing with people.

The doors are closed, no one is left outside. A few minutes later the five foolish girls arrive, breathless. Their lamps now shine with burning, flickering flames. But it's too late. They knock and speak these anguished words: "Sir, open up, we beg of you!" Silence. "Please open the doors, it's us!" A voice is heard: "Who are you? Never heard of you..."

We can just imagine the expression on the faces of those five girls: "Never heard of us? But he invited us himself... It can't be possible!"

The sounds of the party going on inside must have destroyed them with longing. Hell must be just like this: not being there; there where joy reigns.

The parable ends with a piece of advice, repeated elsewhere in the Gospel: "Watch out, because you do not know the day or the hour."

I mentioned earlier that the end is less explicit than in other parables: arriving late is one thing, but not turning up at all is something else. The desire to meet the groom still burned in the five excluded girls. They took things too lightly and their sin was one of lack of foresight.

In other words, there is no harsh and final sentence. Even the curt "never heard of you" could be interpreted as an invitation to try again, perhaps next September, as though this was not their moment. They had to wait, and purgatory is waiting, a "limited" punishment. I say this because I am sure that, during the party, the five wise girls put in a good word for their unfortunate friends in the knowledge that the groom, on his wedding day, couldn't refuse to do something for them. Because heaven has its own dynamics of love, the solidarity of a large family (with its theological language, the Church calls it "communion of the saints"). Those who are joyful cannot be totally disinterested in those who wait outside the door. For this reason, turning to Our Lady, the saints and those who have gone before us has a meaning.

Our real problem is always being ready for the call, casting a light of faith and hope over the mystery of death (the lamps of our soul should never run out of this oil).

When speaking of Don Bosco, occasional fun

was made of the "exercise of good death" which he taught his pupils every month. There's nothing funereal in this practice. Instead, it is an extraordinary lesson in Christian reality, learned in time (that is, in childhood) so that, as adults, we can look at this event with the eyes of one who believes and hopes. As for the rest, let's leave it to God's infinite mercy.

An invitation
from God

Once more Jesus spoke to them in parables, saying: "The kingdom of heaven may be compared to a king who gave a wedding banquet for his son. He sent his slaves to call those who had been invited to the wedding banquet, but they would not come. Again he sent other slaves, saying, 'Tell those who have been invited: Look, I have prepared my dinner, my oxen and my fat calves have been slaughtered, and every-thing is ready; come to the wedding banquet.' But they made light of it and went away, one to his farm, another to his business, while the rest seized his slaves, mistreated them, and killed them. The king was enraged. He sent his troops, destroyed those murderers, and burned their city. Then he said to his slaves, 'The wedding is ready, but those invited were not worthy. Go therefore into the main streets, and invite everyone you find to the wedding banquet.' Those slaves went out into the streets and gathered all whom they found, both good and bad; so the wedding hall was filled with guests.

But when the king came in to see the guests, he noticed a man there who was not wearing a wedding robe, and he said to him, 'Friend, how did you get in here without a wedding robe?' And he was speechless. Then the king said to the attendants, 'Bind him hand and foot, and throw him into the outer darkness, where there will be weeping and gnashing of teeth.' For many are called, but few are chosen."

(Matthew 2:1-14)

Then Jesus said to him, "Someone gave a great dinner and invited many. At the time for the dinner he sent his slave to say to those who had been invited, 'Come; for everything is ready now.' But they all alike began to make excuses. The first said to him, 'I have bought a piece of land, and I must go out and see it; please accept my regrets.' Another said, 'I have bought five yoke of oxen, and I am going to try them out; please accept my regrets.' Another said, 'I have just been married, and therefore I cannot come.' So the slave returned and reported this to his master. Then the owner of the house became angry and said to his slave, 'Go out at once into the streets and lanes of the town and bring in the poor, the crippled, the blind, and the lame.' And the slave said, 'Sir, what you ordered has been done, and there is still room.' Then the master said to the salve, 'Go out into the roads and lanes, and compel people to come in, so that my house may be filled. For I tell you, none of those who were invited will taste my dinner.'"

(Luke 14:16-24)

There are two versions of this story in Matthew and Luke. Matthew adds two dramatic scenes, left out by the other evangelist. A comparative reading of both texts helps us to understand the differences in character and style of the two narrators.

Matthew was once a tax collector, a classic muscle-man used to straight talking. Luke, on the other hand, was a doctor and one of Paul's companions during his missionary journeys. He was very refined and a painter of some talent, to whom more than one portrait of the Virgin Mary is attributed. His style of writing resembles that of an alert modern-day reporter.

Let us, therefore, draw some comparisons. Matthew speaks of a king who gives a gala banquet to celebrate his son's wedding. The *crème de la crème* both of nobility and the world of finance always attended such functions. It is always a grand occasion when a prince and heir to the throne takes a wife.

The king stands on ceremony, and sends messengers to deliver the invitations. However, what happens next is not what you would expect from the usual society news reports of such occasions. While there are people who would give anything to be present at such a banquet (just to say "I was there"), in this case nobody wanted to go.

In Luke's story, the host was not a king, but simply a man who gives a big dinner party. The guests in this version also turn down the invitations, but they do it tactfully. One explains that he has just bought a farm and needs to check that all is in order; another has to try out five pairs of oxen recently bought. They are both well-mannered and beg the messenger to excuse them to his master. The third seems to have a better excuse to stay at home: he has recently married and is still on honeymoon.

Either way, both the king and the man take offence. But the king doesn't lose his temper and sends his servants back again to renew the invitation. Yet another refusal. Some make themselves scarce, leaving word that they are in the country; others make a display of how busy they are in their shops; and lastly there are those – the worst, the "big shots" who are used to making their own decisions – who grab hold of the servants, insult them and then kill them.

Now the king "is angry" and sends in his troops to wipe out the murderers and raze their properties to the ground. It was a lightning strike, a *blitz* as we would call it today.

The celebration must go on regardless. The meal is ready and all that paraphernalia can't be just thrown away. The king lets his servants loose on the streets to invite anyone they meet to the party, the "good and the bad" as Matthew says. While Luke is more specific: "tramps, cripples, the blind", the dregs of society with no one to care for them. "Come on, there's plenty of room", the waiters say, but there are still empty place-settings. So more servants are sent out into the country-side ("along the hedges", as Luke says) with the task of "forcing people to come" so that the dining hall will be full. "Doctor Luke" ends his story with a bitter picture of the host: "None of those men who were invited, I tell you, will taste my dinner."

As for Matthew's king... He is satisfied with having filled his dining hall and goes to greet the guests. He gladly shakes their hands. Then, his expression suddenly changes. He saw a man who was not wearing wedding clothes (the king had ordered a new suit of clothes to be given free for the occasion). In all probability, this man had come in through a side entrance instead of the main door. "Friend," says the king, "how did you get in here without wedding clothes?" He waits for a reply, any excuses, but none are forthcoming. The stranger remains silent. He is immediately sentenced: "Tie him up hand and foot, and throw him outside in the dark. There he will weep and gnash his teeth (a typical way of describing desperation in those days). For many are invited, but few are called."

The final blow goes to a small group of listeners who are too interested by far in the parable: the Pharisees. Matthew, who had associated with them in the past and knew them well, concludes: "They went off and made a plan to trap Jesus with their questions."

The meaning of some of the rather mysterious verses of this story can be found in the invitation. God invites us to celebrate with him. His first invitations go to the elite and, as always happens in the Gospel, they let him down. Sooner or later, their behaviour is punished (the glutton, for example) or scolded (like the priest and the Levite in the story of the good Samaritan). However, if we take a good look at ourselves in the mirror, we can identify with this élite, rejected by Jesus. We receive the invitation when we are baptised. We belong to the fortunate category who receive the invitation first. The king's servants are the Church ministers who tell us of this divine offer. In fact, through baptism and the other sacraments, God calls us by name to his feast. From this point of view, the reference to the Eucharist, the feast which most closely resembles the parable banquet, is too clear for words.

However, our response is too often that polite reply described by Luke: indifference. We don't appreciate the extraordinary meaning of the absolutely free gift we are given. So much so that we give far more importance to dedicating our time to business, social life and success. When faced with a choice between a football match and Mass (an invitation to dinner from Jesus Christ), most of us make straight for the stadium.

Nonetheless, God has incredible patience with those who behave in this way. Although turned down and ignored, he bounces back. There are times when suffering, illness or great sorrow cause us to feel the emptiness of this way of life. These things remind us that money, business deals and the high life do not bring happiness. And when we feel this emptiness inside, it's as though the king's messenger has come to knock at the door to invite us to the party.

The borderline case is that of those who were annoyed by the king's insistence. They take it out on his servants by mistreating and even killing them. This is often the bitter destiny of the prophets, as well as the history of our time.

However, I would like to linger a little over the episode of the "intruder" who entered the dining hall without the proper wedding clothes. At first glance, the wretched man deserves a bit of sympathy. After all, he didn't turn down the invitation and went to the party. Perhaps he was a late-comer who, not wanting to make a bad impression, slipped in through the tradesman's entrance in the hope of not being noticed among all his table-companions. But it all went wrong. The king's calling was not haphazard, but a personal calling to be taken seriously. Just because you are in the dining hall doesn't mean you have a right to eat.

Everything changes once you have been allowed in. And it is no accident that the king calls the stranger "friend". Acceptance (through the words of the godparents) of the invitation offered at baptism, and registration with the Church, is not enough in itself. This suit or clothing which assures us of God's friendship must also change our description. Metaphors aside, it is clear that we must convert because all are invited but not all are chosen. The Gospel is demanding. We have seen it many times and this pitiless fact proves it.

Being left out of the banquet means being left outside the Kingdom. Neither Gospel story tells us what happened to the first to be invited, except for the harsh punishment inflicted on the murderers who killed the king's servants. But it isn't difficult to imagine what happened. For them – the indifferent – there is silence and exclusion, darkness and weeping like the intruder who was thrown out. In other words, unhappiness. Because without God, happiness is an impossibility. Don't believe all those pseudo guests who continuously bombard us all day long. They make too many promises they are not capable of keeping. None of them have the right answers regarding our final destiny.

Not refusing the invitation repeatedly offered by the king is, therefore, much more than a matter of politeness. It is wisdom. Ignoring it, on the other hand, would be suicide.

Love betrayed

When Jesus entered the Temple, the chief priests and the elders came up to him as he was teaching, and Jesus told them: "Listen! There was a landowner who planted a vineyard, put a fence around it, dug a wine press in it, and built a watchtower. Then he leased it to tenants and went to another country. When the harvest time had come, he sent his slaves to the tenants to collect his produce. But the tenants seized his slaves and beat one, killed another, and stoned another. Again he sent other slaves, more than the first; and they treated them in the same way. Finally he sent his son to them, saying, 'They will respect my son.' But when the tenants saw the son, they said to themselves, 'This is the heir; come, let us kill him and get his inheritance.' So they seized him, threw him out of the vineyard, and killed him. Now when the owner of the vineyard comes, what will he do to those

86

tenants?" They said to him, "He will put those wretches to a miserable death, and lease the vineyard to other tenants who will give him the produce at the harvest time."

Jesus said to them, "Have you never read in the scriptures:

'The stone that the builders rejected
   has become the cornerstone;
this was the Lord's doing,
   and it is amazing in our eyes'?

Therefore I tell you, the kingdom of God will be taken away from you and given to a people that produces the fruits of the kingdom. The one who falls on this stone will be broken to pieces; and it will crush anyone on whom it falls."

When the chief priests and the Pharisees heard his parables, they realized that he was speaking about them. They wanted to arrest him, but they feared the crowds, because they regarded him as a prophet.

(Matthew 21:23,33-46)

The parable about the betrayal of love – as we can most definitely call it – is one which must have deeply touched Jesus while he told it. In fact, it symbolises the bitter prophecy of his suffering (Passion). The main character in this parable is not a king or master, but a "father with a family". Jesus uses these very words, even though the story is not about a father/son relationship.

This father accomplishes a project which seems to have been very important to him: he plants a vineyard (no doubt with the finest vines), surrounds it with a hedge, installs a wine-press and erects a tower in the middle. When everything is ready, he sends a group of tenant-farmers to work there. Then he goes far away. It is the artificial re-enactment of creation: the Father, who made the world, wants it to be habitable. The vines, the hedge, the wine-press and the tower symbolise the activities of the people who cultivate the earth, take the produce and look after it. In other words, they live off it.

Having entrusted his property to the tenants, the owner "goes far away". This is a recurring theme in the Gospel parables and its meaning is extremely clear: God entrusts us with the task to be carried out in accordance with his plan and then takes a back seat. He wants to see what we make of it. He gives the responsibility to us.

There is also an emphasis on matters of eco-logical importance. The earth is given to us on trust for our own use. And yet, the destruction wreaked on our planet by modern "civilisation" in the name of "progress" is obvious to everyone. Just look at any one of the many rivers flowing near industrial cities. You can't even see the water for the amount of discharged foaming scum. Fish are dying in the lakes through lack of oxygen. Aqueducts have to be disinfected with chlorine so the water can be drinkable. Weed-killers sprayed on fields are poisoning even the edible mush-rooms and the air we breathe is polluted by clouds of gas from cars and chemical plants. The Chernobyl nuclear disaster told us the dramatic truth about millions of people who died of cancer as a direct result of radioactive contamination. Not to mention the deserts implacably advancing in areas where there was once fertile soil.

We really do have to ask ourselves if this earth of ours still resembles the vineyard which the Creator gave us to cultivate.

Having dealt with this ecological diversion, let's see what's happening in our story. At harvest time, the family man sends his servants to collect the grapes and the wine. Then something unforeseen happens: the tenants don't want to know. They are the sort of people who only understand the language of violence. The first servant is brutally beaten, the second (who, perhaps, was too insistent about his master's rights being respected) was killed. The third was stoned.

The family man is shocked. However, he thinks that the tenants will change their minds if he sends a larger number of servants. But it was wishful thinking, and the same thing happens again. At this point, this Father displays boundless patience. He makes a strange decision. He is convinced that if he sends his son, the tenants will show more respect and give in. But the tenants were behaving like veritable gangsters, and he hadn't realised how wicked they really were. "This is the owner's son and heir," they said, "if we get rid of him, the vineyard will automatically become ours." Premeditated murder. And sure enough, as soon as the son arrives, he is captured, taken out and killed. Here Jesus must have paused for quite a while, and an expression of tragic awareness must have flashed across his face. And yet he is at the height of his popularity. He has just made his triumphant entry into Jerusalem, cheered by an enormous crowd. He had driven the money-lenders out of the temple and had performed miraculous cures. Soon he was to be hated for unleashing his decisive attack on the hypocrisy of the ruling class.

Just as everyone was anxious to hear the end of the story, the Teacher asks someone else to tell it. Before him stood a group of priests and elders with whom he had just had a lively debate. They had asked him what right he had to teach the people, and he had replied with a question: "Where did John's baptism come from, heaven or man?" This had really put them on the spot, and they were forced to reply: "We don't know." He asked them a rhetorical question: "Now, when the owner of the vineyard comes" – this time Jesus uses the word "owner" and not "father" – "what will he do with those tenants?" The answer was taken for granted: "He will certainly kill those evil men, and rent the vineyard to other tenants who will give him his share of the harvest at the right time."

Jesus not only accepts this conclusion, but enforces it with a quote from the Scriptures: "The stone which the builders rejected as worthless turned out to be the cornerstone." And to clarify his meaning: "And so I tell you, the kingdom of God will be taken away from you and be given to a people who will produce fruits. Whoever falls on this stone will be broken to pieces; and if the stone falls on someone it will crush him."

The priests and elders realised that he was referring to them. They would have liked to arrest him but they were afraid of the people's reaction. However, their revenge was only postponed.

When St Jerome commented on this exchange of remarks, he gave it a precise meaning: the vine is the people of Israel, the tenants are the priests and Levites, the servants are the prophets. (Is it just a coincidence that Jeremiah was beaten, Isaiah killed and Zechariah stoned?) The argument is just the same when applied to us: the vine is the wealth of faith and the world which Christ has given to the Church for conversion. Or, at a lower level, it is the theorem of existence that the Father has given us to resolve; the gift to be made to flourish (remember the talents?). We should all examine our conscience and think about the "vine" that we have been given to cultivate, because we all have to reckon with the Father. No one can say "this is my life, my body belongs to me, the world is mine to do with as I see fit" – all sayings dear to today's radical culture. But none of the things we see around us truly belong to us. We can actively use them, but we only have them for safe-keeping.

The families we raise, the politician's responsibility to the public; these are also vines. During our lifetime, we are all tempted to take something that doesn't belong to us, to behave as though the "Father of the family" doesn't exist. However, he has only "distanced" himself, and now and then sends his servants to demand some produce. How many prophets have been rejected or even killed – even among today's Christians! In recent history, "Christian" Europe looked on with great indifference as six million Jews were systematically exterminated. Any voice raised in objection to the crime was eliminated: a Carmelite priest, Tito Brandsma, was injected with a lethal substance in Dachau because he continued to write courageous anti-Nazi articles for the Catholic press. And to think, while all this was going on, our schools were teaching their pupils that blacks were an inferior race which needed to be "civilised" by us!

It's true that Christians in the West had been given the task of spreading their wealth of faith to make it flourish. Perhaps Jesus' prediction is being verified today: "The kingdom of God will be taken from you and given to a people who will produce the proper fruits." It is no accident that seminaries and formation houses for religious in Africa and certain countries in the East and Latin America are full to overflowing, while we have a continuous vocation crisis. Our society is more and more decided to put God into "oblivion". A society which rejects the Father's servants and even kills his Son. In fact, the Jesus we read about in the Gospel actually died because the person presented to us by literature, political ideology, entertainments and even some Christians themselves is not the Christ-God in whom we believe, but just a Man even if spelled with a capital M: a political agitator, a marvellous healer, an eminent philosopher, a generous philanthropist, a charismatic public speaker or even a myth. In other words, a shadow of the real Jesus of Nazareth. A Jesus who does not rise from the dead is nothing other than a famous figure no longer living.

So keep an eye on the vine, and lend an ear to the servant-prophets (including the saints, whom the Church quite rightly calls God's servants) who remind us of our duty. Otherwise, the end could be as bitter as in other parables. For those with a hard heart, the patient "family man" will turn into a just and relentless master.

God's patience

One day Peter asked Jesus, "Lord, if my brother sins against me, how often should I forgive? As many as seven times?" Jesus said to him, "Not seven times, but I tell you, seventy-seven times.

"For this reason the kingdom of heaven may be compared to a king who wished to settle accounts with his slaves. When he began the reckoning, one who owed him ten thousand talents was brought to him; and, as he could not pay, his lord ordered him to be sold, together with his wife and children and all his possessions, and payment to be made. So the slave fell on his knees before him, saying, 'Have patience with me, and I will pay you everything.' And out of pity for him, the lord of that slave released him and forgave him the debt. But that same slave, as he went out, came upon one of his fellow slaves who owed him a hundred denarii; and seizing him by the throat, he said, 'Pay what you owe.' Then his fellow slave fell down and pleaded with him, 'Have patience with me, and I will pay you.' But he refused; then he went and threw him into prison until he would pay the debt. When his fellow slaves saw what had happened, they were greatly distressed, and they went and reported to their lord all that had taken place. Then his lord summoned him and said to him, 'You wicked slave! I forgave you all that debt because you pleaded with me. Should you not have had mercy on your fellow slave, as I had mercy on you?' And in anger his lord handed him over to be tortured until he would pay his entire debt. So my heavenly Father will also do to every one of you, if you do not forgive your brother or sister from your heart."

(Matthew 18:21-35)

Once upon a time there was a king. We really should call him "the King", with a capital letter. As the protagonist of many of Jesus' parables, he is presented as an absolute ruler with power over life and death. We know that he is God, by whom we are judged at the end of our existence. A just King but also (and above all) an infinitely good King.

This parable of denied forgiveness touches on a sore point: the hardened heart, a sore point that is far more widespread than we might think if we

95

were to examine our consciences faithfully and courageously. In it we find a telling comment on the verse in the "Lord's Prayer" that says: "Forgive us our trespasses, as we forgive those who trespass against us."

There is good reason why this story appears in the Gospel according to Matthew (the only place where it does appear). It was inspired by a question asked by Peter, and perfectly in character with his sanguine temperament: "Lord, how many times must I forgive my brother if he sins against me? Seven times?" To him, this already seems plenty, but Jesus says: "No, not seven times, but seventy times seven," which could be taken to mean seven to the power of seventy: an enormous number, equivalent to infinity, meaning always.

As he confided in Jesus, Peter (who had probably been wronged by someone) may well have thought: "Patience has a limit." However, Jesus clearly states that patience must have no limits, must be infinite and eternal like God's patience. There must be forgiveness. Only on this condition can we, in turn, be forgiven by the Lord. A sort of law of retaliation in reverse. In the Gospel, many things appear to be the opposite from the usual opinion of society. "Love your enemies, be kind to those who hate you, bless those who curse you, pray for those who slander you... What merit is there in loving only those who love you? Even if sinners do it."

Since, in all probability, Peter was not very convinced by his reply, Jesus explained by telling the story of the unforgiving servant.

Once again the main character is a dishonest manager. The king asks one of his ministers to report to him. While going over the accounts, he discovers a deficit of ten thousand talents, an astronomical sum when compared to its value today. The deficit incurred by this minister (probably the governor of one of the provinces in the kingdom) could even be compared to the entire budget of one of our counties today. But perhaps Jesus exaggerated the sum so that we would understand that our debt with God – our sin – is always huge because it offends the Infinite, the Absolute.

The minister cannot justify the colossal shortfall. He had probably invested the public money in his private business. Once again it's like reading a news report today, with the exception that the sentence was immediate and there were no "boards of inquiry" to shelve the case or cause delays. The king ordered his guilty servant to be sold together with his wife and children (let's not forget that we are his property). He was totally ruined. Not even the rest of his life was long enough for him to make amends.

The desperate minister saw all his mistaken speculation collapse like a house of cards. He knows his days are numbered, so he plays his last card. He is very familiar with his sovereign and knows him to be soft-hearted as well as just. He throws himself at his feet, crying and begging for his patience, assuring him that he will repay the whole amount. The king is moved by this "scene" (perhaps thinking of the wretched man's wife and children), and not only orders the guards to set him free but also forgives the entire debt. How true it is that God's mercy has no bounds. His forgiveness is total.

However, it is here that we discover the true nature of this minister. He is a swindling liar, a born actor who, knowing the king's weakness, played a crafty game to get what he wanted. He goes off bowing and scraping, but all the while thinking to himself: "He fell for it, the blockhead, and my money is safe and sound..." He is hard-hearted and utterly selfish, and shows it straightaway. As soon as he is outside, he meets a subordinate who owes him one hundred denarii (about forty gold sovereigns). He grabs him by the scruff of his neck, almost strangling him, and shouts: "You crook! Give me my money back or I'll throw you into gaol!" The other man throws himself to the ground and begs him to wait. The minister doesn't listen to reason. The law he had broken can become sacred if it suits him. He calls the police and imprisons the poor man. "You won't get out until you've paid back the last penny!"

We are still in the palace. Some of the king's other officers, who had witnessed the scene and were probably friends of the second debtor, run straight to the king and spill the beans. They can't wait to see the bully get his come-uppance.

The end is tragic: the minister hasn't had time to turn the corner before being seized by the guards and taken back to the throne room. Now the tune is played quite differently. The king simply sentences him with a few, very severe words: "I forgave you your debt because you asked me. Should you not also have had mercy for your fellow servant, just as I had mercy for you?" He doesn't even wait for an answer. "And he handed him over to the torturers," the Gospel says, while Jesus comments tersely: "That is how my Father in heaven will treat you if you do not forgive your brother from your heart." If we take Jesus' words at face value, some observations immediately spring to mind.

1. We have to pay a price for God's mercy on us: our mercy on others. And it's not an optional ten thousand talents for one hundred denarii. A Christian cannot tell himself this if he does not fully accept this logic of love. Jesus gives a paradoxical example: "To the person who strikes you on the cheek, turn the other cheek. To the person who takes away your cloak, allow him to also take your suit. Give to whomever asks you. And do not ask him to return it." Quite frankly, we are tempted to say, this is carrying things a bit too far: "I'm nobody's fool..." And yet, we have no other choice if we want to deserve complete forgiveness. Of course, this reasoning does not mean we can't defend ourselves, especially self-defence. But we must never use violence. The roots of true pacifism are contained in these words. (Gandhi had understood; in his heart he was undoubtedly a Christian.) They also contain the teaching on correct application of human justice: violence never pays, as our own era has clearly demonstrated.

2. Why have mercy? Because none of us can ever probe into the souls of those who hurt us. For this reason, during the funeral of the girl who was killed in the bombing at Enniskillen, her father forgave. We must never forget that even the most hardened criminal can redeem himself. Mercy is more than justice. Perhaps when the world ends, we will discover that this is where true justice lies. Another reason why the death penalty makes no sense, at least from a Christian point of view.

3. Where people are concerned, we still find those who grab the debtor "by the scruff of his neck", forgetting that history has forgiven the creditors for far worse crimes. So much is said about Third World debts, and those of the poor South when compared to the industrialised North on this planet. The World Bank asks for money and threatens not to grant any more loans until those already granted have been repaid. This is capitalist logic, the unyielding law of economics.

But the North forgets that it was the first to invade those lands, often exterminating the inhabitants to take possession of their natural resources (it's still happening in some areas of Latin America). It is the industrialised countries (for the most part calling themselves Christian) who exploit the poor countries – as we have already said – in so many ways, with no regard for their territory and their cultural heritage. The king mentioned in the Gospel – the Lord of history – will also demand an explanation for this plundering.

4. Jesus invites us to forgive "with our hearts". We often hear the phrase "I will forgive, but I will never forget" which, in practice, means "I don't feel like forgiving". That "with the heart" means that it is necessary to forget everything and forever, bury the hatchet, start again from the beginning with those who have harmed us as though nothing had ever happened. It's not easy, but a Christian has to aim at this. Before he died on the cross, Christ reminded us of this with his very human appeal to the Father: "Forgive them for they know not what they do."

Lastly, the parable gives us a valid reason to forgive by reminding us that we all – to a greater or lesser extent – owe something to God and to others. And so? So when Jesus invited anyone who was without sin to cast the first stone at the adulteress about to be stoned to death, the entire area surrounding him and the woman was vacated within a matter of minutes. Everyone left, starting with the oldest. At least as far as they were concerned, they had understood that condemning and sentencing was no longer a right and that forgiving was a duty. Then and there the world entered a new era.

God
never says no

Jesus was praying in a certain place, and after he had finished, one of his disciples said to him, "Lord, teach us to pray, as John taught his disciples." He said to them, "When you pray, say:

> 'Father, hallowed be your name.
>> Your kingdom come.
> Give us each day our daily bread.
> And forgive us our sins,
>> for we ourselves forgive everyone indebted to us.
> And do not bring us to the time of trial.'"

And he said to them, "Suppose one of you has a friend, and you go to him at midnight and say to him, 'Friend, lend me three loaves of bread; for a friend of mine has arrived, and I have nothing to set before him.' And he answers from within, 'Do not bother me; the

102

door has already been locked, and my children are with me in bed; I cannot get up and give you anything.' I tell you, even though he will not get up and give him anything because he is his friend, at least because of his persistence he will get up and give him whatever he needs.

So I say to you: Ask, and it will be given you; search, and you will find; knock, and the door will be opened for you. For everyone who asks receives, and everyone who searches finds, and for everyone who knocks, the door will be opened. Is there anyone among you who, if your child asks for a fish, will give a snake instead of a fish? Or if the child asks for an egg, will give a scorpion? If you then, who are evil, know how to give good gifts to your children, how much more will the heavenly Father give the Holy Spirit to those who ask him!"

(Luke 11:1-13)

We not only ask God for forgiveness, but also for help. It only stands to reason. Jesus often prayed alone, and the disciples were curious to know what on earth he was saying when he was alone. One day they asked him: "Teach us to pray, just as John taught his followers." And so we have the Lord's Prayer which, in a few lines, summarises the basic order of creation. It contains everything: the right things to want, the wrong things to avoid, the correct path to follow and the means to be used to lead a truly Christian life.

However, having offered us this "magic formula" for life, Jesus still urges us to always turn to the Father with all the persistence and trust of a child. He does this by telling two stories.

A man had to offer hospitality to a friend who unexpectedly arrived on his doorstep late at night, but he had no food in the house. What should he do? It's midnight and the shops are closed. He had no choice but to knock at his neighbour's door and ask if he could borrow a few loaves of bread. The annoyed neighbour replied: "Fancy coming in here at this hour of the night! The children are in bed and I can't start rummaging through the house." However, the man insisted: "I'm sorry, but I am making such a bad impression on my guest. You're a fine friend..."

In the end the poor old neighbour, probably cursing him under his breath, put his slippers on and gave him all the bread he wanted. In other words, as Jesus says, knock and the door will be opened (even reluctantly), ask and you will receive, seek and you will find. We need to be go-getters, and at times we need the cheek of a door-to-door salesman who manages to twist the arm of the most obstinate housewife. He goes on to say that if a neighbour gives you what you want, even if just to get you out from under his feet, think how much more generous your heavenly Father will be.

Jesus hammers home the comparison: "Would any one of you fathers give his child a stone when he asks for bread? Or a snake when he asks for fish? Or a scorpion when he asks for an egg? As bad as you are, you know how to give good things to your children. To an even greater extent, the Father in heaven will give the Holy Spirit to those who ask him!"

This is the keystone of correct prayer: ask God for the "Holy Spirit". We forget it all too often. We usually only turn to God when we are in trouble and need something. How many (useless) prayers are said to win the lottery or the football pools! When we are sick, we beg to get better and the good Lord often answers our prayers. But no one ever thinks about asking for the gift of faith, for the strength to live a Christian life – for the Holy Spirit.

Having clarified how and what we need to ask in our prayers, we come to the second story which urges us to persist with God "without ever becoming discouraged". There is this judge. He is reluctant to give judgement in favour of a poor widow who has been wronged. The accused must have been a big-shot, a boss, and the judge obviously doesn't want to get in his bad books so he continuously postpones the conclusive hearing.

In the Jewish community at that time, this sort of woman was considered to be very weak because a female without a husband had no legal rights. Nevertheless, the widow does not give in. She was especially strong-willed because she knew she was right. As soon as she had some free time, she ran to the court to see if it was her turn. "Give my adversary what he deserves", she begs. The judge always finds an excuse to postpone the hearing, but as more and more time passes the more this episode becomes a nightmare for him. Eventually he makes up his mind: "Even though I have no fear whatsoever of God, or anyone else for that matter, this woman won't leave me alone. I'll give her her due just to get her off my back."

Persistence, that's the answer... insistence and courage. Justice can prevail, even for helpless widows. It has been known to happen.

To get back to the parable... If a poor woman can force a judge to do his duty, there's even greater reason for God to listen "to his chosen people who call to him day and night".

Pay attention though, because the end seems to disclaim all the earlier affirmations. Jesus looks around and asks: "When the Son of Man comes, will he find faith on earth?"

I venture to say that he will. When, for example, I read about those "chosen people who call to him day and night" appealing for mercy for everyone, I think of all the thousands of monks and cloistered nuns all over the world. These hallowed souls offer up their prayers and receive unimaginable grace from God. They are obvious proof of the faith; they guarantee its continuity, its foundation. They are the yeast that secretly, and mysteriously, changes humanity. And, thank heaven, it seems that the more our society tends towards the secular, towards distancing itself from God, the more this vocation grows.

True confession

Jesus also told this parable to some who trusted in themselves that they were righteous and regarded others with contempt:

"Two men went up to the temple to pray, one a Pharisee and the other a tax collector. The Pharisee, standing by himself, was praying thus, 'God, I thank you that I am not like other people: thieves, rogues, adulterers, or even like this tax collector. I fast twice a week; I give a tenth of all my income.' But the tax collector, standing far off, would not even look up to heaven, but was beating his breast and saying, 'God, be merciful to me, a sinner!'

I tell you, this man went down to his home justified rather than the other; for all who exalt themselves will be humbled, but all who humble themselves will be exalted."

(Luke 18:9-14)

This is one of the most courageous parables told by Jesus, because it exposes the ambiguities of the controlling ruling class with its finger firmly on the button of power.

By speaking these words, Jesus probably signed his own death warrant. For some time now, he had been stepping up his attacks on the scribes and Pharisees and had clearly expressed his opinion of them: "You are the ones who want to appear before men as the just, but God knows your mistakes because that which is honourable among men is abomination in God's eyes!" On another occasion he was even harsher: "You wash the outside of your glass and your plate, but the inside is full of plunder and wickedness." He called them "hypocrites", "blind guides", "like whited sepulchres that appear splendid from the outside but, inside, are full of dead bones and all manner of decayed matter", "snakes, vipers". This series of "compliments" caused him to be hated by them all.

So two men go up to the temple to pray. They appear to be doing the same thing, but they each have a different relationship with God just as their state of mind is different. One of them, the Pharisee, was an observant follower. In any case, this was imposed upon him by his rank. Of course, it is much easier to obey the law when you have the security of a good family, education, career, prestige and power. Another reason why prisons are almost always full of poor people.

The other man however was a publican, one of the tax collectors working for the Romans, and especially hated by the people because they served the invader and mostly as thieving loan-sharks.

The Pharisee begins by thanking God "for not being like the others". He is a racist. The roots of that modern-day heresy called "apartheid" are buried deep within his way of thinking. There are still many people who behave this way today, and not just in South Africa. There are those who, for example give a wide berth to the Gipsies who – they say – are nothing but swindling robbers. They generalize, just like the Pharisee who took one look at the tax collector, probably a total stranger, and contemptuously cast his judgement.

He was "standing up", probably in the first row among the notables, praying "to himself" without even moving his lips and behaving as though he was top of the class. He thanks God that he is "not like all the others, the greedy, dishonest, the adulterers", and not like "that tax collector over there" either. Then he goes on to list his merits: "I fast two days a week, I pay out one tenth of all my income." In itself, this would be a point in his favour. He is not a tax evader, which the publican probably is. But he ruins everything with his "I am this and I am that." Quite the "modest" man!

His is a strange way of praying. Instead of prostrating himself before the Lord of the universe and measuring his insignificance as a man against God's mercy, the Pharisee takes careful note of his own superiority. A far cry from the Lord's Prayer, the model prayer taught to us by Jesus himself. But we understand the reasons: he is more concerned with saving face and making a public display of going to the temple to pray. As if it were enough just to go to church (often simply a social convention) in order to be a true Christian. We know it's not like that, although in some cases we might get the impression that people who don't go to church are better than some church-goers. When a poor person swears, it is often the result of ignorance, and not so much aimed at God as at people and a community where lack of concern for his needs perpetuates the unfairness.

Those who do not know love and understanding allow themselves to be guided by prejudice. This is confirmed in one episode of the Gospel where Jesus is having dinner in the home of a Pharisee called Simon. A woman comes in, a known prostitute in the town. She bathes Jesus' feet with her tears and dries them with her hair after perfuming them with precious oil. Simon's prejudice immediately springs into action: "If he were a prophet, he would know what sort of woman she is, what race she belongs to (an ill-fated choice of words) and that she is a sinner." He doesn't actually say this, he just thinks it but Jesus reads his mind and shows him up with: "Her many sins have been forgiven because she has shown so much love."

We return to the temple and move from the front row towards the back where we find the tax collector. He stands apart, not even daring to raise his eyes towards heaven, but beats his breast and says: "Oh God, have pity on me for I am a sinner!"

This is a true confession, spoken out loud and

with a gesture which Christian liturgy will later adopt at the beginning of the celebration of Mass with the words: "I have sinned through my own fault." The tax collector is realistic and presents himself properly before the Lord. Although certainly not a regular "church-goer", when he does decide to go to the temple he does it with a sincere heart. All he wants is for God to listen to him, and he is not ashamed of his own moral shortcomings. We are not told what it was that pushed him into it, but it seems certain that he must have been up to something and wanted to lift the pangs of guilt from his conscience. There is nothing better than kneeling in a confessional to square accounts with one's conscience.

In the gospels we come across another tax collector who invited Jesus and the disciples to dinner in his home. "Many tax collectors and sinners came and were sitting with him and his disciples", writes Matthew explaining that these people were fairly unreliable.

Zacchaeus was also a tax collector. However, he did not meet God's divine grace on the way to the temple in Jerusalem, but in Jericho as he was climbing a sycamore tree (he was not a tall man), curious to get a better view of the Jesus everyone was talking about. Once again, when Jesus told him that he would like to eat at his house, the "thinkers" found fault: "He is a guest in the home of a sinner." However, what they didn't know was what happened immediately afterwards: "standing before the Lord", Zacchaeus was suddenly converted. Unscrupulous people like him don't like half measures or pretence, whatever they may be doing: "Listen, Lord! I will give half of my belongings to the poor, and if I have cheated someone, I will repay him four times as much." No sooner said than done.

Jesus himself tells us how God answered the prayers of the two main characters in the parable: "I tell you that this man [the tax collector] was in the right when he went home, unlike the other. For he who makes himself great will be humbled and he who is humble will be made great."

Luke adds a conclusive epilogue to his story. This time the "thinkers" are some of the disciples. While Jesus is telling the parable of the Pharisee and the tax collector, some children are brought along to him. The disciples begin to scold the parents, telling them to take the children away. But Jesus intervenes: "Let the children come to me. Do not stop them because the kingdom of God belongs to such as these. In truth I say to you, whoever does not receive the kingdom of God like a child will never enter it."

The important people, the intellectuals, those who hold powerful positions are once again repudiated. Childhood, therefore, is the standard against which our conduct as believers should be measured. Jesus could not have used a better or more easily comprehensible standard, because the young child accepts everything without discrimination of any sort. The "differences" only emerge when we become adults. The child is spontaneous, without malice and incapable of pretence. Children express their inner feelings. When they are in difficulty, they turn to their parents in the knowledge that they will receive help, warmth and forgiveness. In its three sections, the Lord's Prayer expresses the child's loving admiration for his dad, the assurance that he will be given his daily bread and the pledge to deserve it.

The tax collector prayed with the sincerity of a child and, for this reason, he was in the right when he went home. Since we have all done something for which we must ask forgiveness, we must simply do as he did.

Appearances
are deceptive

PARABLE OF THE TWO SONS

When Jesus entered the temple, the chief priests and the elders of the people came up to him as he was teaching and he asked them "What do you think? A man had two sons; he went to the first and said, 'Son, go and work in the vineyard today.' He answered, 'I will not'; but later he changed his mind and went. The father went to the second and said the same; and he answered, 'I go, sir', but he did not go. Which of the two did the will of his father?" They said, "The first."

Jesus said to them, "Truly I tell you, the tax collectors and the prostitutes are going into the kingdom of God ahead of you. For John came to you in the way of righteousness and you did not believe him, but the tax collectors and the prostitutes believed him; and even after you saw it, you did not change your minds and believe him."

(Matthew 21:23,28-32)

114

Appearances are deceptive – a fitting title for this brief parable that touches on something we experience within ourselves every day: the fragility of human nature. In his letter to the Romans (7:14ff), St Paul says: "I do not understand what I do, because I do not do what I want. On the contrary, I do what I do not want."

Jesus sets out the problem using few words. A father asks one of his two sons to go and work in the vineyard. It often happens in family life. Someone is asked to do something, a simple task like getting the bottle of milk from the fridge, going to buy a newspaper, washing the dishes and so on. However, the son must have got out of bed on the wrong side. Perhaps he had already made plans to see his friends that day. Whatever the case may have been, he answered his father with a curt: "I don't feel like it." At least he was honest. Although the good man was hurt, he didn't insist. He was obviously not an authoritarian who demands obedience at all times. Quite apart from which, his son was probably an adult, so using his belt to give him a good hiding wouldn't have helped. Never mind, the head of the family thinks to himself, I can always ask my other son.

Soon afterwards, the same thing happens again. However, this boy is cunning and doesn't say what he thinks. He respectfully answers his father's request: "Certainly, Dad, I'll go to the vineyard right away." A formal act of obedience, but not from the heart (after all, think of how many times subordinates have to say yes to the boss when what they really want to do is politely tell him to buzz off). The sly fellow has already figured out a way to wriggle out of doing the job. He thinks up an excuse and doesn't go to work.

But let's just go back a minute. His brother detected the disappointed look on his father's face. Deep down he was sorry. There are times when children intuitively realise how much Mum and Dad suffer in silence because of them. Sometimes a telling look, a slight grimace or a passing frown is enough for the message to get through. So the boy changes his mind and, without a word, decides to obey his father. He cancels his arrangements and goes to the vineyard where he is surprised not to find his brother.

Jesus asks his listeners a provoking question: "Which of the two did what his father wanted?" They answered: "The first." Good, but now we must draw the conclusions. "In truth I say to you" – an expression used by Jesus when he wanted to say something important – "the tax collectors and the prostitutes will go to the kingdom of God ahead of you. For John came to you showing you the right path to take, and you would not believe him; and even after seeing these things [not long beforehand, Jesus had thrown the money-lenders out of the temple and healed some blind people and cripples] you did not change your minds and believe him."

The Father wants repentance. This is the essence of the parable. How often we find ourselves saying no to the Father. It's part and parcel of the weakness described earlier by St Paul. Often – and we always apply this to others – there are a thousand hidden reasons behind the refusal, showing the complexity of the human heart and the motivation behind every conscious act. This is why we should not judge anyone. Only God can delve into our hearts. Appearances are deceiving and, as in other parables, Jesus asks us to bear this in mind. He purposely chooses the tax collectors and prostitutes – considered to be the "dregs" of society by the conformists in those days – as symbols of those who say "no" and then change their minds, reconfirming that they will go to the kingdom of God ahead of the others.

We can just imagine the expressions on their faces as the people listened to these words. Jesus is basically saying that at least the sinners have watertight excuses: a broken home, bad examples set by parents or their environment, the lack of material and moral support while they were growing up. The others have no excuse. Regardless of the miracles, they did not believe John then, nor do they believe Christ now, and they have not changed their minds.

An even better parallel is drawn in Luke, chapter 7, when Jesus praises John the Baptist in front of the crowd: "What did you expect to see in the desert?" he asks. "So, what did you expect to see? A man dressed in fancy clothes? Those who dress like that and live in luxury are found in kings' palaces [a sensational onslaught on the corruption lurking in the centres of power, the "palaces"]. So, what did you expect to find? A prophet? Yes, I tell you, much more than a prophet..." All the people who had listened, even the tax collectors, obeyed God's righteous demands and were baptised by John. However, by not being baptised by him, the Pharisees and the teachers of the law (those who hypocritically say "yes" to God with words but do the opposite with their actions) rejected the kingdom of God.

Once again therefore, the simple people "and even the tax collectors" follow the voice of heaven, while the learned reject it, and with it their salvation. A very harsh statement. It is a refusal of the Father's persistent invitation. And Jesus concludes: "To whom should I therefore compare the people of this generation and what are they like? They are like children sitting in the market place, calling out to each other and saying: 'We played the flute for you but you would not dance. We sang funeral songs, but you would not cry.'"

Clearly, because of our condition we have no excuse for saying "no" to God. For the most part, we have been born and raised in a Christian environment. Having been baptised, and having been confirmed, we are asked to work in the vineyard. In one way or another, this means witnessing our great faith to others. We solemnly say "yes" but do nothing about it. Often we have to learn kindness, honesty, the courage of those who have much less than we do but who, with the grace of God, are sorry for their previous refusal and God's will is actively "done". We not only risk being overtaken in the kingdom of God (this would be the least of it), but we risk outright exclusion.

Ninety-nineagainst one

PARABLES OF THE LOST SHEEP

At that time the disciples came to Jesus saying, "Who is the greatest in the kingdom of heaven?" And calling to him a child, Jesus put him in the midst of them and said, "Take care that you do not despise one of these little ones; for, I tell you, in heaven their angels continually see the face of my Father in heaven. What do you think? If a shepherd has a hundred sheep, and one of them has gone astray, does he not leave the ninety-nine on the mountains and go in search of the one that went astray? And if he finds it, truly I tell you, he rejoices over it more than over the ninety-nine that never went astray. So it is not the will of your Father in heaven that one of these little ones should be lost."

(Matthew 18:1-3,10-14)

Now all the tax collectors and sinners were coming near to listen to him. And the Pharisees

119

and the scribes were grumbling and saying, "This fellow welcomes sinners and eats with them."

So Jesus told them this parable: "Which one of you, having a hundred sheep and losing one of them, does not leave the ninety-nine in the wilderness and go after the one that is lost until he finds it? When he has found it, he lays it on his shoulders and rejoices. And when he comes home, he calls together his friends and neighbours, saying to them, 'Rejoice with me, for I have found my sheep that was lost.' Just so, I tell you, there will be more joy in heaven over one sinner who repents than over ninety-nine righteous persons who need no repentance.

Or what woman having ten silver coins, if she loses one of them, does not light a lamp, sweep the house, and search carefully until she finds it? When she has found it, she calls together her friends and neighbours, saying, 'Rejoice with me, for I have found the coin that I had lost.' Just so, I tell you, there is joy in the presence of the angels of God over one sinner who repents."

(Luke 15:1-10)

We cannot read certain sections of the Gospel according to Matthew without being especially impressed by the arguments which Jesus put to his listeners. Because of the rapid sequence of extraordinary events and because of their – shall we call it – "singularity", at times they seem to be contrary to common sense (as we have already seen, God's logic is obviously not the same as ours).

We turn to chapter 14: Jesus has performed the amazing multiplication of the loaves and fish. To be precise, he fed five thousand men (without counting women and children) with five loaves and two fish, and twelve baskets were filled with the left-overs. He stood there and single-handedly prepared a colossal picnic.

"Immediately afterwards", the evangelist points out, as the sun is setting and the disciples take the boat out into the lake, a violent wind begins to blow. Jesus reaches them by walking on the water and calms the storm. (There is also a comic interlude when Peter, whom Jesus had called to join him, almost drowns in the waves because of his lack of faith.)

Then we have the second multiplication of the loaves (seven this time, and a few fish to feed four thousand people with seven baskets of left-overs). Without doubt these are amazing events, but events that took place before the people's very eyes. We may be astonished, but it is difficult not to believe in someone who can accomplish such wonders. Then, the exceptional vision of the transfiguration was witnessed by three favoured apostles, but Jesus expressly orders them not to speak of it until after his resurrection.

Then we have some astonishing statements

which must have jolted many a listener: "He who wants to save his life will lose it; but he who loses his life for my sake, will find it." Or else: "If your faith is like the grain of mustard, you will say to this mountain: 'Move from here to there', and it will move and nothing will be impossible for you." And still more: "If your hand or your foot is no good, cut it off and throw it away. You are better to enter life with one hand or one foot, than having two arms and two feet and being thrown into the eternal furnace..." The same is said about eyes.

Lastly, there is a concise yet disturbing announcement: "The Son of Man is about to be handed over to men. They will kill him, but on the third day he will rise again". Strangely, the disciples only dwell on the first part of the message, and forget the second part (the resurrection). In fact, they "were deeply saddened by it".

After a few more remarks, the brief but very beautiful parable of the lost sheep is told. The shepherd, who has one hundred sheep, loses one and leaves the other ninety-nine "on the mountains" to go and look for it. This really doesn't make any sense at all: leaving ninety-nine to go in search of one? We would say it's not worth it because we risk losing the entire flock. But no. It's quite obvious that God (he is the shepherd) cannot allow even one sheep to wander away from the fold. What is more, "If he finds it", Jesus adds, "he will be happier over this one sheep than over the ninety-nine that did not get lost. In just the same way, your Father in heaven does not want any of these little ones to be lost."

Being a journalist, Luke sets the scene "in the desert" rather than on a mountain and goes into great detail to describe the moment when the sheep is found: the "very happy" shepherd puts it on his shoulders and carries it home. He calls his friends and neighbours together to celebrate with him. "In the same way," he explains, "there will be more joy in heaven over one sinner who repents than over ninety-nine respectable people who do not need to repent."

We could end here, but it's well worthwhile lingering a little longer over this unconventional shepherd whose attitude would surely work against him if he were seeking employment. John intervenes to guide us with the only parable in his Gospel, told in his own inimitable way by skipping the details in order to explore the psychology of the main character. He tries to explain the shepherd's reasons for swimming against the stream. He has a special relationship with his sheep, rather like that of a father with his children.

An identikit is drawn so that he can be immediately recognised by his appearance. Jesus says: "He who does not enter the pen through the gate, but climbs over the other side, is a thief and a murderer." There are no half measures. It is vital not to make any mistakes on this count.

Then Jesus adds some important details: "The shepherd opens the door to him, and the sheep hear his voice, and he calls his sheep by name and leads them outside. And when all his sheep are outside, he walks in front of them; and the sheep follow because they know his voice. They would not follow a stranger, but would flee from him because they do not know the voice of strangers."

But the people did not understand, so Jesus had to explain: "I am the gate... whoever passes through me will be saved. He will come in and go out and find the pastures. A thief only comes to rob, kill and destroy. I have come so that they may have life in abundance."

Here, John goes way beyond the other evangelists. He shows us a shepherd who not only goes to look for a lost sheep and celebrates finding it, but he also unveils the mystery of the love that lies at the heart of Christianity. "The good Shepherd gives up his own life for his sheep. The paid hand, who is not a shepherd and to whom the sheep do not belong, abandons the sheep and runs away when the wolf approaches, and the wolf takes the sheep and scatters them. The paid hand flees because he is a mercenary and does not care for the sheep. I am the good Shepherd. I know my own, and my own know me, just as the Father knows me and I know the Father. And I give my life for my sheep." He finishes with a sentence that embraces the entire world and shows that Jesus is truly the Lord throughout history, the ultimate goal: "And I have other sheep, that are not from this fold. I must lead them also and they will listen to my voice, so that there will be only one flock and only one shepherd."

The universal dimension of this prophecy must have dumbfounded the listeners. So much so that some of them, "many of them" in fact, said: "He is possessed by the devil and raving. Why listen to him?" But there were also those who openly and realistically commented: "These are not the words of one possessed. Can a demon open a blind man's eyes?"

The same thing happens today when the Church speaks out. Many people can't be bothered listening to this voice. But the Lord never lets up. A preference for the lost sheep is typical of God. This does not mean that those who are faithful to him are less worthy. On the contrary, their prize will be even greater. However, it is a fact that God doesn't want to leave anyone outside the door to heaven, not even the most hardened criminal.

Luke repeats this concept with his parallel account of the woman who has lost one of her ten silver coins. She lights a lamp and sweeps her house, searching everywhere until, having found it, she rejoices with her friends.

The
logic of love

PARABLE OF THE PRODIGAL SON

Then Jesus said, "There was a man who had two sons. The younger of them said to his father, 'Father, give me the share of the property that will belong to me.' So he divided his property between them.

A few days later the younger son gathered all he had and travelled to a distant country, and there he squandered his property in dissolute living. When he had spent everything, a severe famine took place throughout that country, and he began to be in need. So he went and hired himself out to one of the citizens of that country, who sent him to his fields to feed the pigs. He would gladly have filled himself with the pods that the pigs were eating; and no one gave him anything.

But when he came to himself he said, 'How many of my father's hired hands have bread enough and to spare, but here I am dying of hunger! I will get up and go to my father, and

I will say to him, "Father, I have sinned against heaven and before you; I am no longer worthy to be called your son; treat me like one of your hired hands."' So he set off and went to his father. But while he was still far off, his father saw him and was filled with compassion; he ran and put his arms around him and kissed him. Then the son said to him, 'Father, I have sinned against heaven and before you; I am no longer worthy to be called your son.' But the father said to his slaves, 'Quickly, bring out a robe – the best one – and put it on him; put a ring on his finger and sandals on his feet. And get the fatted calf and kill it, and let us eat and celebrate; for this son of mine was dead and is alive again; he was lost and is found!' And they began to celebrate.

Now his elder son was in the field; and when he came and approached the house, he heard music and dancing. He called one of the slaves and asked what was going on. He replied, 'Your brother has come, and your father has killed the fatted calf, because he has got him back safe and sound.'

Then he became angry and refused to go in. His father came out and began to plead with him. But he answered his father, 'Listen! For all these years I have been working like a slave for you, and I have never disobeyed your command; yet you have never given me even a young goat so that I might celebrate with my friends. But when this son of yours came back, who has devoured your property with prostitutes, you killed the fatted calf for him!'

Then the father said to him, 'Son, you are always with me, and all that is mine is yours.'"

(Luke 15:11-31)

After the fascinating "prologue" of the sheep that was lost and then found, we come to the even more fascinating story of the prodigal son. It is one of the most hopeful stories ever written and, like others in the Gospel, it has all the flavour of a true story. The protagonists are God and man, who are indivisibly linked for all eternity.

Luke unveils the infinite goodness of God, a father hopelessly in love with his children regardless of whether they are good or bad. Some of the parables (as we have seen earlier) have a bitter or even tragic outcome. God's patience is sometimes challenged by human wicked men and so he decides to administer justice. But not here, where fatherly love triumphs over all.

In this story, the father has two sons. The family is well-off and want for nothing. Nevertheless, the younger of the two feels he needs more elbow room. He is a dreamer, and the tranquillity of his humdrum daily existence bores him despite the guarantee of financial security and a loving family. He longs for adventure. Some of his ill-chosen friends are probably leading him astray: "You call this living?" we can hear them say. "Look around, get rid of the monotony, you're an adult now, lead your own life. Or do you still have to ask Daddy if you can stay out late?" The sort of thing we hear from young people today. They are only relatively at fault: rebellion is often encouraged as an expression of creativity, while breaking the law is considered by both secret and dedicated followers of radical-chic to be a conquest. Not only have we lost our sense of sin, but a taste for perversion has crept in. We talk of the "me culture" and the "me generation" where everyone is a law unto himself and makes his own decisions about morality. The result is written all over the newspapers.

Our young man becomes more and more intolerant, clashing with his parents from time to time. The generation gap. Then one fine day he decides to leave home. He asks his father for his share (one third of the inheritance according to local custom, the other two thirds going to the eldest son) and goes away "to a distant land". These words not only reflect his rejection of his family, but the mirage of some sort of happiness. How true it is that we often go to the ends of the earth to find something that was under our noses all the time! But his exhilaration is such that everything seems beautiful. He is "free" at long last! He's got plenty of money and no shortage of friends (hangers-on) fawning all over him. The result: in short, the Gospel says, "he squandered everything and led a dissolute life."

Prison chaplains listen to hundreds of stories like this. We are reminded of the story of Pinocchio who was persuaded to follow Lucignolo to Toyland and soon found himself living like an animal. What else could Collodi's book be but a secular paraphrase of the parable of the prodigal son, where father Geppetto's love wins in the end?

The party is soon over for this young man. Money is running short and friends are making themselves scarce. If you don't work, you don't eat. Moreover, a severe famine spreads over that distant land and our young man is hungry and penniless. Having left home to "live his own life", "find fulfilment" and "find himself" (as many young people say today), away from parental influence, he begins to realise that the easy path only leads to a dead end. Once again, a modern-day picture: when the money runs out, so many young people end up in vice, prostitution, drugs and "low life" from which it is so difficult to escape.

Fortunately, the young man doesn't fall into the trap. He picks up the pieces (some dignity is always left when you come from a good family), and accepts a job looking after a herd of pigs for a local landowner (no Jew, not even the poorest, would ever normally accept such a job because pigs are considered impure and therefore it would be unlawful). He would have eaten the carob beans given to the pigs, but no-one gave him any. He really was in a terrible state. He found his job very tiring because he was half-starved and unused to work. His future was looking frighteningly grim, so he decided to return home. Amid the silent countryside and pangs of hunger he begins to "come to his senses".

To tell the truth, his repentance is a bit "dirty", at least to start with. He never thinks of the pain he has caused his parents by leaving home in that way. His reasoning is rather practical: "My father's workers have plenty of bread to eat, while I am here dying of hunger!"

On the road home he thinks about what he's going to say during the first embarrassing moments of their meeting. They are the words of sincere repentance. He will admit his mistake, not just to his father, but first and foremost to God: "I have sinned against Heaven and against you." It is a recovery of moral awareness. His sense of sin will be accompanied by the words: "I am no longer worthy of being called your son. Treat me as one of your workers."

Sincere words, no doubt about it. However, the son shows that he really doesn't know his father deep down, because his father had never lost hope of embracing him again and has been gazing constantly at the horizon, in total silence.

He walked and walked and, after a few days, he finally came within reach of his father's farm. "He was still a long way off when his father saw him coming," Luke tells us in a masterly manner, "and his heart was filled with pity." The long wait is over. First there is compassion which explodes into joy. The son is exhausted and dirty. His clothes are in rags and he hangs his head in shame. He is defeated. The father doesn't wait for him on the doorstep, but runs towards him, throws his arms around his neck and tenderly kisses him.

Just think of the effect it would have on us if two fine actors played this scene! The father makes the first move. He is the first to forget (not one scolding word is mentioned about what has happened) and the first to make peace. The son doesn't even have time to speak the words he has rehearsed before hearing the head of his family order the servants to fetch new clothes, a ring for his finger and a pair of shoes, and to kill a fat calf for a feast. "For this son of mine was dead, but now he is alive," says the father jumping for joy. "He was lost, but now he is found."

Luke tells us that the celebration began straightaway. Here there is the scene where the older brother takes offence and refuses to enter the house. To his father he says: "I don't understand, I've worked here for years without ever disobeying you, and you've never given me so much as a goat to share with my friends for dinner. This 'gentleman' lost his shirt on women, and when he turns up again you throw a party. A fine fool I've been!"

But the father cuts him short and answers back: "You are always at home, and everything I have is yours. But now we must celebrate, for your brother was dead and now he is alive." As always, God's logic is different from ours. At first glance, we are tempted to side with the older son who has always behaved properly. But then, if we think about it, we come to understand the divine plan: Christ was sent to deliver us from sin. In the Easter liturgy, the Church rightly speaks of original sin as a "happy fault, which gained for us so great Redeemer".

We have so often confessed things like this. We have so often "returned to the Father", sincerely sorry for the wrongs we have committed. In some countries, the practice of confession is believed to be in noticeable decline, if not totally absent. I wonder how we could manage without the inner comfort that absolution can give, the moment when we really feel the embrace and tender kiss of the Father who forgives and orders celebration in heaven. No psychiatrist's couch could ever replace the confessional.

However, we often behave like the older brother. We side with the "good" (remember the Pharisee in the temple?), with "the righteous", and we get angry with the Lord because of his "recoveries" that smack of prodigality. This is God's style. Matthew, Zacchaeus, the Samaritan, Saul of Tarsus, Augustine of Hippo, Ignatius of Loyola and many many more saw the light in the most unimaginable way. The father reminds the eldest son that by staying with him he has everything. He has peace, joy, security and things that are never appreciated until they have unfortunately been lost.

In this regard, we are reminded of the marvellous words written by Primo Mazzolari in his book *The Most Beautiful Adventure*: "It is sad to see our frequent incomprehension of God's infinite generosity, and how it worries, obstructs or outrightly halts the path of those souls searching for God!...The father's love covers them and clothes them after his embrace has restored them inwardly. There are many paths all leading to only one landing place, one port of call: the Church. This is the father's heart, wide open at the end of every path, as love is never behind but always ahead... God's embodiment and suffering are follies of his love so that sinners will accept him. After such a folly, we understand how the greatest sin is not believing in God's love for us."*

*Primo Mazzolari (1890-1959) today considered by many as a forerunner of the Second Vatican Council, was a simple parish priest first in Cicognara and then in Bozzolo, in the diocese of Cremona in the Lombard region of northern of Italy. His work *The Most Beautiful Adventure* (La più bella avventura), a commentary on the Parable of the Prodigal Son, was first banned by the ecclesial authorities because it was too open and conciliatory to those outside or far away from the Church.

Who
is my neighbour?

PARABLE OF THE GOOD SAMARITAN

Just then a lawyer stood up to test Jesus. "Teacher," he said, "what must I do to inherit eternal life?" He said to him, "What is written in the law? What do you read there?" He answered, 'You shall love the Lord your God with all your heart, and with all your soul, and with all your strength, and with all your mind; and your neighbour as yourself." And he said to him, "You have given the right answer; do this, and you will live."

But wanting to justify himself, he asked Jesus, "And who is my neighbour?" Jesus replied, "A man was going down from Jerusalem to Jericho, and fell into the hands of robbers, who stripped him, beat him, and went away, leaving him half dead. Now by chance a priest was going down that road; and when he saw him, he passed by on the other side. So likewise a Levite, when he came to the place and saw him, passed by on the other side. But a Samaritan while travelling came near him; and when he saw him, he was moved with pity. He went to him and bandaged his wounds, having poured oil and wine on them. Then he put him on his own animal, brought him to an inn, and took care of him. The next day he took out two denarii, gave them to the inn-keeper, and said, 'Take care of him; and when I come back, I will repay you whatever more you spend.' Which of these three, do you think, was a neighbour to the man who fell into the hands of the robbers?" He said, "The one who showed him mercy." Jesus said to him, "Go and do likewise."

(Luke 10:25-37)

If the cinema had existed in Jesus' day, this would have been an ideal film script for a director. All the ingredients are there: scenery, adventure, drama and a happy ending.

But there's some doubt about whether the film would have gone down well with the people of Judaea because the "goodie" is a Samaritan. The mere mention of this word made the Jews angry. The Samaritans, the secular enemies of the Jews, were considered to be heretics and excommunicates because they had dared to erect their temple

on Mount Garizim in opposition to that in Jerusalem. In other words, a cursed race to be avoided.

Besides that, when he was talking about this
episode, Jesus had just experienced the hateful
feelings the Samaritans had for their neighbours.
In the passage immediately preceding the parable,
Luke tells this story: "As the time drew near for
Jesus to be taken up, he decided to go to Jerusalem.
He sent some messengers on ahead and they went
into a Samaritan village to make ready for him.
But the people there would not receive him because
he was on his way to Jerusalem."

The apostles were very upset. James and John
even wanted the Lord to teach the "enemies" a
good lesson: "Do you want us to command fire to
come down from heaven and destroy them?" A
very harsh curse indeed. But Jesus rebuked them
and decided to go to another village.

So there was more than one good reason to be
angry with the Samaritans and their unwelcoming
attitude. However, Jesus "took revenge" in his
own way by telling an astounding story. It was the
consequence of a question asked by a "teacher of
the law" (the token intellectual) who decided to
put him to the test: "Teacher, what must I do to
receive eternal life?" Not an easy question, and
quite a gamble. Jesus answered: "What do the
Scriptures say?" The well-read man said: "You
must love your God with all your heart, with all
your soul, with all your strength and with all your
mind; and you must love your neighbour as yourself." "Your answer is correct," replied Jesus, "do
this and you will live."

This seemed to be the end of it, but the man went on and not without a little malice. However, he didn't try to find out what Jesus meant by those four words that seem to have the same meaning (all your heart, all your soul, all your strength and all your mind). What he wanted to know was: "And who is my neighbour?"

Now faced with a proper question (the other one was just a pretext to attack his speech), Jesus replied by telling a story. Where people were concerned, he never spoke in the abstract. He gave practical examples, and this time he even drew on the crime news.

A man was going down from Jerusalem to Jericho. It wasn't an easy journey in those days: twenty-seven kilometres across a sandy desert with high rocky peaks and steep ravines. A Far West landscape starting seven hundred metres from the Holy City and stretching as far as the oasis of Jericho, two hundred and fifty metres below sea level.

We don't know the identity of the traveller. The fact that Jesus did not give him a name could perhaps mean that his mishap could happen to any one of us without distinction. We just have to flick through the newspapers to realise this. Halfway there, he was ambushed. A band of criminals robbed him of all his possessions and, as he had probably attempted to defend himself in some way, they also beat him up and left him for dead when they fled.

Jesus probably read the "teacher's" thoughts, written all over his face: "The bandits were no doubt Samaritans..."; but he continues. Two very respectable people were also travelling the same road, both of them employees of the holy temple: a priest and a Levite. The man who had been robbed tries to attract their attention. "Thank goodness someone is coming", he thinks to himself. However, they show little concern and only glance at him, hurrying on ahead. As the poor man becomes unconscious, he thinks: "For heaven's sake, can't they see I'm dying?"

Perhaps the priest, believing the man to be dead, thought of that clause in the Law prohibiting priests from touching a corpse and the problem of a subsequent seven-day period of impurity. He had an iron-clad excuse. At most he would have shrugged his shoulders and commented: "There's no more respect! What is the world coming to... with the odd exception."

As for the Levite, he was decidedly a coward. He reasons: "What if the bandits are still around? They might attack me. I can't be home late. My wife would be so worried."

A few minutes later, a third man arrived, trotting along on his donkey. He was probably a merchant. Here Jesus livens up the picture and purposely "zooms in" for a close-up of the scene. The man seems to be in a cheerful mood. He had probably clinched a good deal in Jerusalem. Perhaps he was tired and anxious to get home for a hot bath before falling into bed, but as soon as he sees the stranger lying on the ground, he comes to an abrupt stop. Now we have the first "close-up shot" which dumbfounds the listeners gathered around Jesus: he is a Samaritan. (The "teacher" just manages to stifle a grimace of disgust). Luke tells us: "He went up to the man and his heart was filled with pity." The other two had kept a safe distance, but not him. This man wanted to take a close look. He immediately recognises the man as an "enemy" of his people and this could have been the right moment to say: "Just what you deserve, you dirty Jew" (I use the same words we unfortunately still hear nowadays from some Christians). However (once again the zoom lens in action), he dismounts the donkey and, bending over the wretched man who is barely breathing, disinfects his wounds with wine and oil (first aid in those days). Then he bandaged the wounds to stop the bleeding, put the man on the back of his donkey and proceeded on foot.

There were no hospitals in Jesus' day, so the Samaritan went to an inn where he must have been a regular visitor and handed the stranger over to the care of the innkeeper. He gave the innkeeper some money and promised to pay any further costs when he returned. Then he carried on to Jericho (Jesus, the film director, probably paused here for a "pan" shot of the Samaritan riding into the distance).

"Which of these three," Jesus asked the "teacher", "do you think was neighbourly to the man who had been robbed?" The reply: "The one who took pity on him." "Your answer is correct. Go then, and do the same."

Strange. In the first question, asked by the "teacher", the word "neighbour" is used as a substantive noun to mean others, those who live nearby or whom we meet casually. However, in the second question, it becomes an adjective to describe correct conduct towards others. The neighbour exists and daily life offers plenty of opportunity to meet people. But Jesus draws attention to the person who suffers, who is in need because this is how the Christian shows himself to be different: "If you only greet your brothers," he says in his long sermon on the mount, "what more do you do? Don't pagans also do this?"

As obvious as it may seem, it happens. A recent example: one day, in downtown New York, I saw a black drug addict who had cut open a vein with a piece of broken glass. He was pouring with blood as he sat leaning against a wall with his legs outstretched. People were passing him by, stepping over him in order not to trip, walking on in total indifference. "Let's stop, this man is bleeding to death", I said to the friend I was with. "The police will take care of him. Surely someone has called an ambulance", he said. And, in fact, it arrived with all the speed you see in American TV films. Efficient yes, but heartless. I dared to add: "Is it because he's black?" My friend answered: "No, big cities are cruel to everyone. Millions of human beings live on top of each other here. Everyone is 'a neighbour' but no one is 'neighbourly' to those who need help."

It happens here. When we see an accident victim, how often we choose to turn a blind eye so as not to get involved with insurance companies or the police. How often we think up an excuse not to give or lend money to a friend who can't make ends meet, and then not hesitate to spend fifty pounds for a ticket to a football match...

The elderly person living at home who is quite a burden at times is a neighbour. The baby whose "unplanned" arrival upsets all the parents' plans is a neighbour. The handicapped turned away by the social services, the tramp, the man next door with whom we fight at residents' association meetings – they are neighbours. And occasionally, even the needy and defenceless enemy. When the Samaritan "approaches", that is to say, "is neighbourly", he forgets everything to do his duty towards his fellow man.

The parable-film has no ending. For example, it doesn't tell us of the robbed man's amazement when he wakes up in a bed with someone looking after him. What is more, it doesn't tell us how he feels when he learns that his benefactor is a Samaritan. Perhaps Jesus didn't want to further provoke the already shaken sensibilities of his interlocutor by adding an embrace between the two "enemies". And yet, this scene should have been put in for a complete "happy ending". In any case, the Samaritan did not expect any gratitude, and his disappearance without expecting thanks is what makes him so great. The echo of that sound track playing as background music to all these stories about the kingdom remains in our souls. The music is called love.

A JOURNALIST
LOOKS AT
THE LORD'S PRAYER

Italian journalist James Antonellis looks at the spiritual, social and universal implications of the Lord's Prayer with disarming honesty, clarity and charm. At every stage, the author's preoccupation as a journalist makes him search the collective conscience of his profession to see how well or badly the media acquit themselves in acting according to the sentiments of the Lord's Prayer. Here is perhaps a lesson for all the other professions too.

But underneath the author's personal and professional concern to practise what we subscribe to every time we recite the Lord's Prayer, there is the insistent vision of God, whom Jesus has taught us to call Father. Hence the boundlessness of Christian love which embraces every human being as brother or sister, free and equal, never, but never to be treated differently because of race or social status. In this spirit of charity, the author tells us, let us dare to say yet again: Our Father...

ISBN 085439 384 6   144 pp.   £4.95